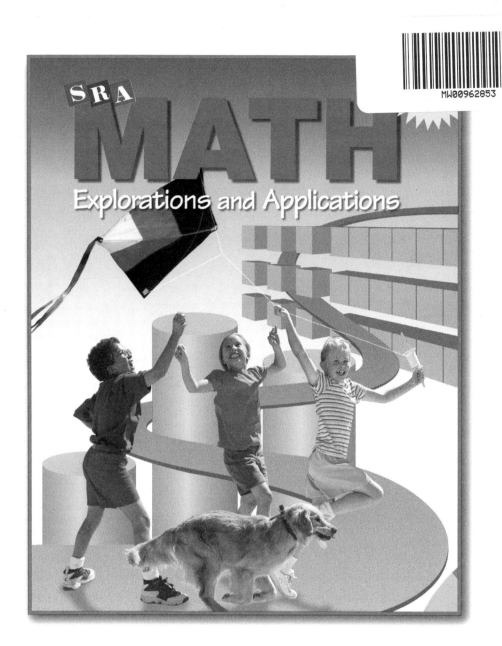

SRA MATH
Explorations and Applications

Stephen S. Willoughby
Carl Bereiter
Peter Hilton
Joseph H. Rubinstein

Columbus, OH

www.sra4kids.com

SRA/McGraw-Hill

A Division of The McGraw·Hill Companies

Copyright © 2003 by SRA/McGraw-Hill. All rights reserved. Except
as permitted under the United States Copyright Act, no part of
this publication may be reproduced or distributed in any form or
by any means, or stored in a database or retrieval system, without
prior written permission from the publisher.

Printed in the United States of America.

Send all inquiries to:
SRA/McGraw-Hill
8787 Orion Place
Columbus, OH 43240-4027

ISBN 0–07–579599–X

2 3 4 5 6 7 8 9 QWD 05 04 03

Contents

UNIT 1 Addition and Subtraction   1

Contents

LESSON

Contents

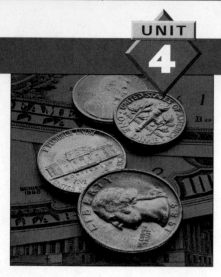

UNIT 1

Addition and Subtraction

REVIEWING AND EXPANDING BASIC FACTS

- fact families
- column addition
- perimeter
- graphing

Farmers use math . . .

Before a farmer or rancher puts up a fence, it is important to figure out how much fence to buy. The length of each side of a field is measured, and the lengths are added together. The fence keeps animals safe and also stops them from eating growing crops.

LESSON 1

Name _____

Counting and Writing Numbers

Roll. Trace or write.

Where are the 3, 4, and 5?

Where are the 8, 9, and 10?

 GAME

Play the "Tracing and Writing Numbers" game.

Trace.

Trace.

Write.

 NOTE TO HOME
Students trace and write the numbers from 0–10 as they play a game.

Unit 1   Lesson 1 • **3**

◆ LESSON 1 Counting and Writing Numbers

If you count the desks, you can estimate how many children are in the class.

Do the "Estimating" activity.

Count.

1 What objects did you count? _____

2 How many? _____

Estimate.

3 What objects will you estimate? _____

4 How many did you estimate? _____

Check your estimate.

5 How many objects did you count? _____

NOTE TO HOME
Students count and estimate, then check their estimates.

LESSON
2

Name _____

More Counting and Writing

Count up or count down. Fill in the missing numbers.

1 | 5 | 6 | | | 9 | | | 12 |

2 | | | 2 | 3 | 4 | | | 7 |

3 | 20 | 21 | | | | 25 | | 27 |

4 | 76 | 77 | | | | | 82 | 83 |

5 | 39 | 38 | | | | | 33 | 32 |

6 | 63 | | 61 | | | | 57 | 56 |

NOTE TO HOME
Students name missing numbers from 0–100.

GAME

◆ **LESSON 2** More Counting and Writing

Counting and Writing Numbers

Players: **Two**

Materials: **Pen and paper for each player**

RULES

First Round

Leader: Choose a starting number and an ending number between 0 and 100.

Leader: Count on from the starting number. Say and write one, two, or three numbers. Then stop.

Players: Take turns counting, saying, and writing the next three numbers.

Winner: The player who says and writes the ending number wins the first round.

More Rounds

The second player becomes the leader, then the third player, and so on.

NOTE TO HOME
Students count and write numbers between 1 and 100.

LESSON 3

Name _____

Counting and Regrouping Money

Work these problems.

How much money?

1    $ _____

2   $ _____

3  $ _____

4   $ _____

NOTE TO HOME
Students review counting money amounts.

◆ **LESSON 3   Counting and Regrouping Money**

Solve these problems.

How much money?

5  _____¢

6  _____¢

7  $_____

8  $_____

Talk about the Thinking Story
"Measuring Bowser."

Play the "Yard Sale" game.

NOTE TO HOME
Students review counting money amounts.

LESSON
4

Name _____

Numbers on the Calendar

December has 31 days.

Fill in the missing numbers.

			December			
Sunday	Monday	Tuesday	Wednesday	Thursday	Friday	Saturday
	1	2	3	4	5	6
7						

Write the answers.

1. What day is December 5? _____Friday_____

2. What day is December 12? _____

3. What day is December 23? _____

4. What day is December 17? _____

NOTE TO HOME
Students fill in missing dates on a calendar and name
specific days of the week.

◆ **LESSON 4   Numbers on the Calendar**

October has 31 days.

Fill in the missing numbers.

October

Sunday	Monday	Tuesday	Wednesday	Thursday	Friday	Saturday
		7				
					24	

Write the day of the week.

5 October 1 _____   **6** October 2 _____

7 October 14 _____   **8** October 9 _____

9 October 17 _____   **10** October 16 _____

11 On October 7 Sam found out that he
would have a test on October 14. How
much time does Sam have to prepare? _____

Play the "Calendar" game.

NOTE TO HOME
Students fill in missing dates on a calendar
and name specific days of the week.

LESSON
5

Name _____

Writing Numbers

Count up or count down. Fill in the
missing numbers.

1 | 3 | 4 | | | 7 | | 9 |

2 | 22 | 21 | | | 18 | | 16 |

3 | 100 | | | | | | 94 |

4 | 54 | 53 | | | | | 48 |

5 | 28 | | | | 32 | | 34 |

6 | | | | 39 | | | 42 |

NOTE TO HOME
Students fill in missing numbers before and after
numbers between 0 and 100.

Unit 1   Lesson 5 • **11**

◆ LESSON 5 Writing Numbers

Mr. Gonzales is 34 years old.

7 How old will he be in two years? _____

8 How old will he be in three years? _____

9 Mark earned two dollars today. Now he has 85 dollars. How many dollars did he have yesterday? _____

10 A train going from Omaha to New York City had 73 cars. Two cars were removed in Chicago and one car was added in Pittsburgh. How many cars reached New York City? _____

11 An airplane holds 67 passengers, two pilots, and one attendant. How many people does it hold all together? _____

NOTE TO HOME
Students solve short word problems.

LESSON 6

Name _____

Adding and Subtracting by Counting

Draw a ring around the answers.

1 21 + 3

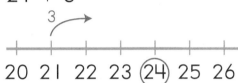

20 21 22 23 (24) 25 26

2 21 − 3

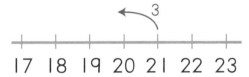

17 18 19 20 21 22 23

3 21 − 2

17 18 19 20 21 22 23

4 19 + 2

18 19 20 21 22 23 24

5 30 + 2

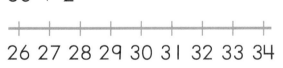

26 27 28 29 30 31 32 33 34

6 30 − 2

26 27 28 29 30 31 32

7 43 + 0

40 41 42 43 44 45 46 47

8 49 + 1

47 48 49 50 51 52 53

9 51 − 2

48 49 50 51 52 53 54 55

10 47 − 0

45 46 47 48 49 50

NOTE TO HOME
Students use number lines to add and subtract
0, 1, 2, or 3.

◆ **LESSON 6** Adding and Subtracting by Counting

Solve these problems. Watch the signs.

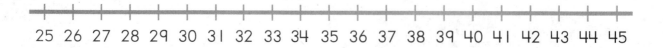

⑪ 31 + 2 = _____   ⑫ 40 − 1 = _____

⑬ 38 + 3 = _____   ⑭ 30 − 1 = _____

⑮ 40 + 1 = _____   ⑯ 29 + 2 = _____

⑰ 35 − 2 = _____   ⑱ 37 − 1 = _____

⑲ 27 − 2 = _____   ⑳ 36 + 2 = _____

㉑ 39 + 2 = _____   ㉒ 42 + 3 = _____

㉓ 33 + 3 = _____   ㉔ 42 − 3 = _____

㉕ 34 + 1 = _____   ㉖ 32 − 3 = _____

NOTE TO HOME
Students add and subtract
0, 1, 2, or 3 using a number line.

LESSON 7

Name _____

Counting Up or Down

Draw a ring around the answers.

1 53 + 2

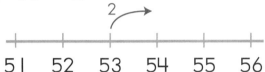

51 52 53 54 55 56

2 42 − 3

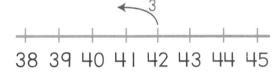

38 39 40 41 42 43 44 45

3 58 + 2

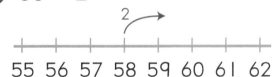

55 56 57 58 59 60 61 62

4 15 + 1

12 13 14 15 16 17 18 19

5 87 − 2

83 84 85 86 87 88 89 90

6 12 − 3

8 9 10 11 12 13 14 15

7 60 − 1

56 57 58 59 60 61 62 63

8 89 + 3

86 87 88 89 90 91 92 93

9 26 + 3

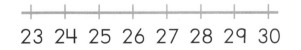

23 24 25 26 27 28 29 30

10 21 − 0

18 19 20 21 22 23 24 25

NOTE TO HOME
Students review using number lines to add and
subtract 0, 1, 2, or 3.

◆ LESSON 7 Counting Up or Down

Solve these problems. Watch the signs.

⑪ 87 + 2 = _____   ⑫ 88 + 3 = _____

⑬ 38 − 3 = _____   ⑭ 32 − 3 = _____

⑮ 48 + 0 = _____   ⑯ 11 − 2 = _____

Use play money to act out the stories.
Write the answers.

⑰ I had $43.
If I spend $2 for a toy,
how much money will I have? $_____

⑱ José is 3 centimeters taller than Len.
Len is 97 centimeters tall.

How tall is José? _____ centimeters

⑲ I had 19¢.
If my sister gives me 3¢,
how much money will I have? _____¢

16 • Addition and Subtraction

NOTE TO HOME
Students solve problems in which they
must add or subtract 0, 1, 2, or 3.

LESSON 8

Name _____

Addition Facts

Add.

1 10 + 5 = _____

2 4 + 4 = _____

3 10 + 8 = _____

4 5 + 5 = _____

5 7 + 10 = _____

6 3 + 3 = _____

7 2 + 10 = _____

8 4 + 3 = _____

9 10 + 9 = _____

10 6 + 10 = _____

11 0 + 10	**12** 5 + 4	**13** 10 + 4	**14** 3 + 10

Play the "Frog Pond" game.

NOTE TO HOME
Students add and play a game using addition facts.

◆ LESSON 8   Addition Facts

Solve these problems

15 There are six cupcakes in each package.
How many cupcakes in both packages? _____

16 Seven children are
on each team. How
many on both teams? _____

17 The ride can hold 12 people. Nine people
are on the ride now. How many more can ride? _____

Save energy—smile! It takes 20 muscles
to frown, but only 14 to smile.

NOTE TO HOME
Students solve word problems.

LESSON 9

Name _____

Double Addends to Ten

Add.

1 4 + 4 = _____

2 2 + 2 = _____

3 3 + 3 = _____

4 5 + 5 = _____

5 9 + 9 = _____

6 7 + 7 = _____

7 8 + 8 = _____

8 6 + 6 = _____

9 0 + 0 = _____

10 1 + 1 = _____

 NOTE TO HOME
Students practice doubling numbers.

◆ **LESSON 9   Double Addends to Ten**

Add.

⑪   4 + 4 = _____   ⑫ 2 + 2 = _____

⑬   10 + 10 = _____   ⑭ 2 + 3 = _____

⑮   9 + 10 = _____   ⑯ 8 + 8 = _____

⑰   9 + 9 = _____   ⑱ 7 + 10 = _____

⑲   4 + 4 = _____   ⑳ 7 + 7 = _____

㉑   4 + 5 = _____   ㉒ 6 + 6 = _____

㉓   5   ㉔   5   ㉕   6   ㉖   3   ㉗   9
    + 5   + 3   + 4   + 3   + 1

㉘   1   ㉙   2   ㉚   7
    + 1   + 4   + 3

NOTE TO HOME
Students practice addition facts.

LESSON 10

Name _____

Addition Facts Review

Add.

1 10 + 7 = _____

2 10 + 10 = _____

3 9 + 7 = _____

4 10 + 9 = _____

5 10 + 5 = _____

6 4 + 10 = _____

7 9 + 5 = _____

8 4 + 9 = _____

9 8 + 10 = _____

10 6 + 10 = _____

11 8 + 9 = _____

12 6 + 9 = _____

13
```
    3
+  10
-----
```

14
```
   10
+   2
-----
```

15
```
    1
+  10
-----
```

16
```
   10
+   0
-----
```

NOTE TO HOME
Students practice addition facts up to 20.

Unit 1   Lesson 10 • **21**

◆ **LESSON 10   Addition Facts Review**

Add.

17 5 + 9 = _____   **18** 7 + 9 = _____

19 5 + 5 = _____   **20** 8 + 8 = _____

21 9 + 9 = _____   **22** 9 + 3 = _____

23 9 + 8 = _____   **24** 3 + 8 = _____

25   6   **26**   9   **27**   3   **28**   6
      + 6   + 6   + 5   + 9
   ————   ————   ————   ————

29   2   **30**   9   **31**   2   **32**   4
      + 9   + 1   + 6   + 9
   ————   ————   ————   ————

There are about 45,000 thunderstorms
in the world every day.

NOTE TO HOME
Students practice addition facts up to 20.

LESSON 11

Name _____

Commutative Property

Add.

1 $10 + 3 =$ _____

2 $6 + 4 =$ _____

3 $3 + 10 =$ _____

4 $4 + 6 =$ _____

5 $8 + 3 =$ _____

6 $2 + 9 =$ _____

7 $3 + 8 =$ _____

8 $1 + 8 =$ _____

9
$$\begin{array}{r} 1 \\ + 10 \\ \hline \end{array}$$

10
$$\begin{array}{r} 10 \\ + 1 \\ \hline \end{array}$$

11
$$\begin{array}{r} 8 \\ + 5 \\ \hline \end{array}$$

12
$$\begin{array}{r} 5 \\ + 8 \\ \hline \end{array}$$

13
$$\begin{array}{r} 9 \\ + 4 \\ \hline \end{array}$$

14
$$\begin{array}{r} 4 \\ + 9 \\ \hline \end{array}$$

15
$$\begin{array}{r} 7 \\ + 6 \\ \hline \end{array}$$

16
$$\begin{array}{r} 6 \\ + 7 \\ \hline \end{array}$$

NOTE TO HOME
Students use the commutative
property to help solve problems.

◆ **LESSON 11 Commutative Property**

What comes out?

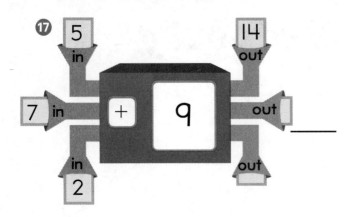

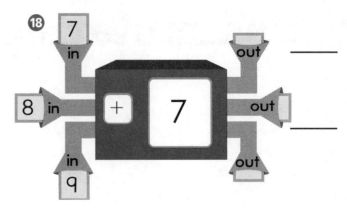

What went in?

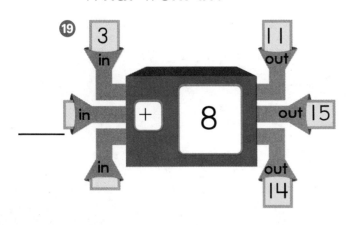

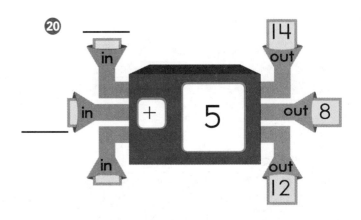

What is the rule?

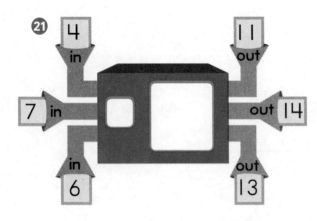

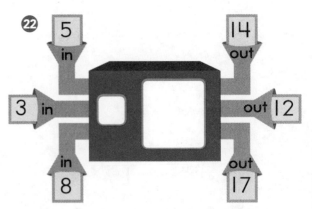

NOTE TO HOME
Students solve function problems.

LESSON 12

Name _____

Reviewing Addition Facts

Add.

① $7 + 8 = $ _____   ② $6 + 7 = $ _____

③ $9 + 8 = $ _____   ④ $5 + 6 = $ _____

⑤ $5 + 7 = $ _____   ⑥ $9 + 7 = $ _____

⑦ $8 + 10 = $ _____   ⑧ $8 + 6 = $ _____

⑨ $9 + 5 = $ _____   ⑩ $9 + 3 = $ _____

⑪ $\begin{array}{r} 7 \\ +9 \\ \hline \end{array}$ ⑫ $\begin{array}{r} 4 \\ +9 \\ \hline \end{array}$ ⑬ $\begin{array}{r} 8 \\ +4 \\ \hline \end{array}$ ⑭ $\begin{array}{r} 7 \\ +4 \\ \hline \end{array}$

⑮ $\begin{array}{r} 6 \\ +9 \\ \hline \end{array}$ ⑯ $\begin{array}{r} 9 \\ +10 \\ \hline \end{array}$ ⑰ $\begin{array}{r} 10 \\ +10 \\ \hline \end{array}$ ⑱ $\begin{array}{r} 10 \\ +3 \\ \hline \end{array}$

Draw a ring around a problem on this page. Write in your Math Journal how you solved it.

NOTE TO HOME
Students review adding nine, adding doubles, doubles plus one, and doubles plus two.

◆ **LESSON 12** **Reviewing Addition Facts**

Add.

19 3 + 5 = _____   20 8 + 3 = _____

21 8 + 1 = _____   22 5 + 8 = _____

23 2 + 8 = _____   24 8 + 2 = _____

25 6 + 4 = _____   26 4 + 6 = _____

27 3 + 7 = _____   28 4 + 7 = _____

29 2 + 7 = _____   30 9 + 8 = _____

31 4 + 9 = _____   32 6 + 2 = _____

33 3 + 2 = _____   34 5 + 1 = _____

35 7 + 1 = _____   36 7 + 3 = _____

The sugarcane plant can grow
to be 20 feet tall.

NOTE TO HOME
Students continue addition practice.

LESSON
13

Name _____

Addition Table

+	0	1	2	3	4	5	6	7	8	9	10
0	0	1	2	3	4	5	6	7	8	9	10
1	1	2	3	4	5	6	7	8	9	10	11
2	2	3	4	5	6	7	8	9	10	11	12
3	3	4	5	6	7	8	9	10	11	12	13
4	4	5	6	7	8	9	10	11	12	13	14
5	5	6	7	8	9	10	11	12	13	14	15
6	6	7	8	9	10	11	12	13	14	15	16
7	7	8	9	10	11	12	13	14	15	16	17
8	8	9	10	11	12	13	14	15	16	17	18
9	9	10	11	12	13	14	15	16	17	18	19
10	10	11	12	13	14	15	16	17	18	19	20

$$5 + 6 = 11$$

Add.

1. $3 + 9$

2. $6 + 5$

3. $8 + 5$

4. $4 + 7$

5. $3 + 6$

6. $8 + 8$

7. $7 + 7$

8. $6 + 6$

9. $9 + 9$

10. $5 + 5$

🎒 **NOTE TO HOME**
Students use an addition table to help them remember
addition facts.

◆ **LESSON 13   Addition Table**

Add.

11 8 + 7 = _____   **12** 7 + 8 = _____

13 2 + 8 = _____   **14** 9 + 4 = _____

15 4 + 9 = _____   **16** 8 + 2 = _____

17 6 + 8 = _____   **18** 8 + 6 = _____

19 3 + 8 = _____   **20** 8 + 3 = _____

21 6 + 6 = _____   **22** 5 + 9 = _____

23 7 + 5 = _____   **24** 7 + 4 = _____

25 9 + 3 = _____   **26** 3 + 9 = _____

27 3 + 4 = _____   **28** 5 + 2 = _____

Play the "Addition Table" game.

NOTE TO HOME
Students continue to practice and play
a game reviewing addition facts.

LESSON 14

Name _____

Practicing Addition Facts

Add.

① 0 + 7 = ____   ② 3 + 6 = ____

③ 9 + 2 = ____   ④ 4 + 8 = ____

⑤ 1 + 8 = ____   ⑥ 7 + 4 = ____

⑦ 10 + 4 = ____   ⑧ 3 + 7 = ____

⑨ 7 + 10 = ____   ⑩ 5 + 8 = ____

⑪ 6 + 6 = ____   ⑫ 8 + 3 = ____

⑬ 5 + 7 = ____   ⑭ 4 + 7 = ____

⑮   6   ⑯   3   ⑰   7   ⑱   9   ⑲   10
   + 8   + 8   + 6   + 9   + 1
   ———   ———   ———   ———   ———

NOTE TO HOME
Students review and learn new addition facts.

◆ LESSON 14 Practicing Addition Facts

Solve these problems.

20 I had four books. I got
three more for my birthday.

Now I have _____ books.

A ball costs $7.
A bat costs $3.

21 How much do they
cost all together? $_____

22 How much do
two bats cost? $_____

23 How much do two balls cost? $_____

24 The soccer team has
won 12 games this season.
If they win three more games
this week, how many games
will they have won so far?   _____

NOTE TO HOME
Students solve word problems.

LESSON **15**

Name _____

Addition Fact Review

ALGEBRA READINESS

What comes out?

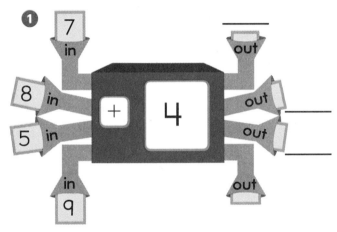

1
7 in
8 in
5 in
in 9
+ 4
out ___
out ___
out ___
out ___

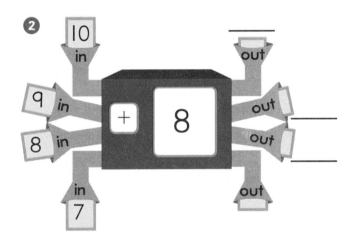

2
10 in
9 in
8 in
in 7
+ 8
out ___
out ___
out ___
out ___

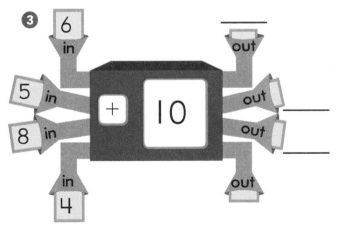

3
6 in
5 in
8 in
in 4
+ 10
out ___
out ___
out ___
out ___

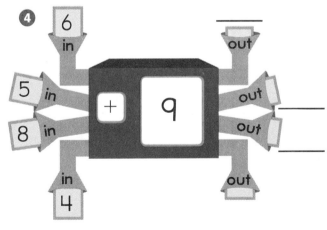

4
6 in
5 in
8 in
in 4
+ 9
out ___
out ___
out ___
out ___

NOTE TO HOME
Students solve function problems.

◆ **LESSON 15** **Addition Fact Review**

Answer these questions.

⑤ How much does the red book cost? $_____

⑥ How much do the red and
blue books cost together? $_____

⑦ How many books are there all together? _____

⑧ How much do the blue and
yellow books cost together? $_____

⑨ How much do the red and
yellow books cost together? $_____

⑩ How much do the three books cost together? $_____

Most dollar bills wear out within two years.

32 • Addition and Subtraction

NOTE TO HOME
Students solve word problems.

LESSON 16

Name _____

Additional Practice

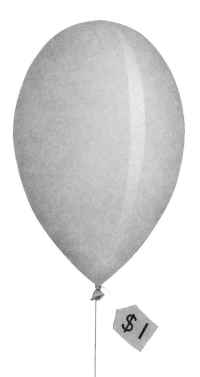

Answers these questions.

1 How much does the toy clock cost? $_____

2 How much do the clock and balloon cost? $_____

3 How much do the doll and clock cost? $_____

4 How much do the clock and doll cost? $_____

5 How much do the clock and tea set cost? $_____

6 How much do the balloon and tea set cost? $_____

7 How much do the tea set and doll cost? $_____

NOTE TO HOME
Students solve word problems.

◆ **LESSON 16 Additional Practice**

Answers these questions.

I have $17.

⑧ Can I buy the clock? _____

⑨ Can I buy the clock and tea set? _____

⑩ Can I buy the clock, tea set, and balloon? _____

⑪ Which three things can I buy? _____

⑫ Can I buy two dolls? _____

⑬ Can I buy two clocks? _____

⑭ Can I buy two tea sets? _____

⑮ Can I buy two balloons? _____

NOTE TO HOME
Students solve word problems.

34 • Addition and Subtraction

LESSON 17

Name _____

Addition Checkpoint

Check your math skills.

1. 0 + 8 = _____

2. 9 + 9 = _____

3. 6 + 6 = _____

4. 3 + 7 = _____

5. 7 + 6 = _____

6. 6 + 8 = _____

7. 9 + 2 = _____

8. 1 + 5 = _____

9. 3 + 6 = _____

10. 10 + 10 = _____

11. 8 + 8 = _____

12. 7 + 2 = _____

13. 7 + 9 = _____

14. 2 + 9 = _____

15. 10 + 4 = _____

16. 9 + 8 = _____

17. 6 + 9 = _____

18. 8 + 4 = _____

Number correct

□

NOTE TO HOME
Students check their knowledge of addition facts.

Unit 1   Lesson 17 • **35**

◆ LESSON 17 Addition Checkpoint

Answer these questions.

$3

$8

$9

$4

19 How much do two paintbrushes cost? $_____

20 How much do two boxes of crayons cost? $_____

21 How much do two packs of clay cost? $_____

22 How much do a set of paints
and another paintbrush cost together? $_____

23 How much do a box of crayons
and a pack of clay cost together? $_____

24 How much do all
the things cost together? $_____

25 How much do crayons
and paints cost together? $_____

NOTE TO HOME
Students solve word problems.

36 • Addition and Subtraction

LESSON 18

Name _____

Subtraction Involving 0, 1, and 2

Subtract.

1 8 – 8 = _____

2 13 – 13 = _____

3 9 – 9 = _____

4 9 – 0 = _____

5 8 – 7 = _____

6 10 – 10 = _____

7 8 – 6 = _____

8 9 – 2 = _____

9 10 – 9 = _____

10 9 – 7 = _____

11 10 – 1 = _____

12 9 – 8 = _____

13 14 – 0 = _____

14 5 – 3 = _____

15
  7
– 2
——

16
  10
– 2
——

17
  9
– 1
——

18
  8
– 2
——

19
  6
– 5
——

NOTE TO HOME
Students review subtraction facts involving 0, 1, and 2.

◆ **LESSON 18**   Subtraction Involving 0, 1, and 2

Solve the problems.

20   8 + 5 = _____

21   3 + 7 = _____

22   4 + 7 = _____

23   6 + 4 = _____

24   6 + 9 = _____

25   5 + 5 = _____

26   10 + 7 = _____

27   9 + 5 = _____

28   5 + 7 = _____

29   9 + 9 = _____

30   $\begin{array}{r} 4 \\ -4 \\ \hline \end{array}$

31   $\begin{array}{r} 10 \\ -8 \\ \hline \end{array}$

32   $\begin{array}{r} 4 \\ +8 \\ \hline \end{array}$

33   $\begin{array}{r} 7 \\ -6 \\ \hline \end{array}$

34   $\begin{array}{r} 7 \\ -0 \\ \hline \end{array}$

35   $\begin{array}{r} 6 \\ -1 \\ \hline \end{array}$

36   $\begin{array}{r} 5 \\ -2 \\ \hline \end{array}$

37   $\begin{array}{r} 4 \\ -3 \\ \hline \end{array}$

GAME

Play the "Roll a 15" game.

NOTE TO HOME
Students review addition facts.

LESSON
19

Name _____

Missing Addends

ALGEBRA
READINESS

Solve these problems.

1 3 + ☐ = 8

2 7 + ☐ = 14

3 ☐ + 5 = 8

4 4 + ☐ = 14

5 9 + ☐ = 15

6 ☐ + 10 = 14

7 8 + ☐ = 15

8 8 + ☐ = 16

9 4 + ☐ = 11

10 ☐ + 9 = 18

11 ☐ + 8 = 11

12 10 + ☐ = 15

COOPERATIVE LEARNING   Do the "Missing Addend Puzzle" activity.

NOTE TO HOME
Students find missing addends in addition sentences.

◆ **LESSON 19 Missing Addends**

GAME

Missing Numbers

Players:	Two or more
Materials:	Two 0–5 Number Cubes and two 5–10 Number Cubes

RULES

Leader: The leader secretly rolls any two cubes and shows one to the other player. Then the leader tells the player the sum.

Players: The player figures out the number that is hidden.

I played the game with

_____.

NOTE TO HOME
Students solve missing addend problems.

LESSON 20

Name _____

Functions

What went in?

1
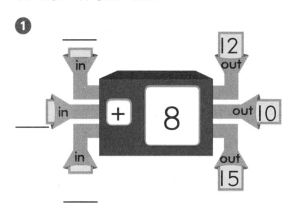

2
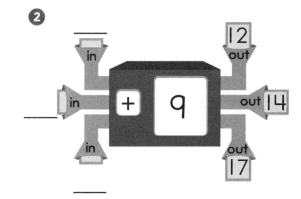

What's the rule?

3
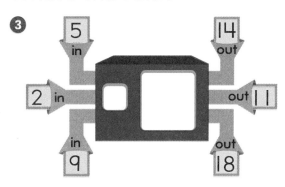

4
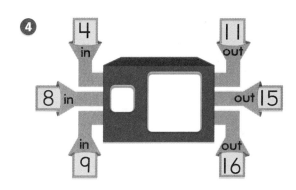

What comes out?

5
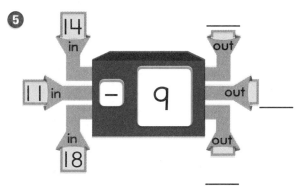

6
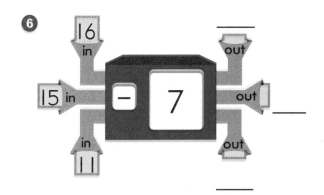

NOTE TO HOME
Students solve function problems involving
addition and subtraction.

◆ **LESSON 20 Functions**

Solve these problems.

7 $2 + \boxed{} = 11$

8 $\boxed{} + 3 = 11$

9 $4 + \boxed{} = 11$

10 $\boxed{} + 5 = 11$

11 $6 + \boxed{} = 11$

12 $\boxed{} + 7 = 11$

13 $11 - 4 = \boxed{}$

14 $11 - 9 = \boxed{}$

15 $11 - 2 = \boxed{}$

16 $11 - 6 = \boxed{}$

17 $5 + \boxed{} = 14$

18 $\boxed{} + 6 = 14$

19 $7 + \boxed{} = 14$

20 $10 + \boxed{} = 14$

21 $\boxed{} + 10 = 14$

22 $14 - 10 = \boxed{}$

23 $14 - 4 = \boxed{}$

24 $14 - 6 = \boxed{}$

25 $14 - 8 = \boxed{}$

26 $14 - 7 = \boxed{}$

Talk about any patterns you see.

NOTE TO HOME
Students practice addition and subtraction facts.

UNIT 1

Name _____

Mid-Unit Review

Count up or down. Fill in the missing numbers.

1 | 7 | 8 | | 10 | | | 13 |

2 | 31 | 32 | | | | 36 | | 38 |

3 | 47 | 46 | | | 43 | | | 40 |

4 | 52 | 51 | | | | 47 | | 45 |

Add or subtract. Watch the signs.

5 24 + 2 = _____

6 35 + 3 = _____

7 29 − 1 = _____

8 49 + 2 = _____

9 42 − 3 = _____

10 30 − 1 = _____

Solve these problems.

11 There are five children on a team. How many children are on two teams? _____

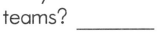

NOTE TO HOME
Students review unit skills and concepts.

◆ UNIT 1 Mid-Unit Review

A hat costs $4. Gloves cost $6.

12 How much do a hat and gloves cost together? $_____

13 How much do two hats cost? $_____

14 How much do two pairs of gloves cost? $_____

Add.

15 3 + 7 = _____   **16** 0 + 9 = _____

17 6 + 5 = _____   **18** 8 + 4 = _____

Solve these problems.

19 3 + ☐ = 12   **20** 4 + ☐ = 12

21 ☐ + 5 = 12   **22** ☐ + 6 = 12

Solve these problems.

23 Jamal had 12¢. He gave his sister 5¢. How much does he have left? _____¢

24 Rita had four fish. Then she got five more. How many fish does she have now? _____

NOTE TO HOME
Students review unit skill and concepts.

LESSON
21

Name _____

Missing Addends and Subtraction

ALGEBRA READINESS

Find the missing numbers.

1 [ ] + 5 = 10

10 − 5 = _____

2 [ ] + 7 = 8

8 − 7 = _____

3 6 + [ ] = 16

16 − 6 = _____

4 [ ] + 7 = 15

15 − 7 = _____

5 [ ] + 7 = 14

14 − 7 = _____

6 [ ] + 4 = 12

12 − 4 = _____

7 5 + [ ] = 14

14 − 5 = _____

8 [ ] + 9 = 13

13 − 9 = _____

THINKING STORY

Talk about the Thinking Story
"Mr. Muddle Takes a Test."

NOTE TO HOME
Students review finding missing addends and use
answers to complete subtraction sentences.

Unit 1   Lesson 21 • **45**

◆ **LESSON 21** **Missing Addends and Subtraction**

Find the answer.

9 The plate and pitcher cost $17.
How much does the pitcher cost? $_____

10 If you have $10 can you
buy a cup and a pitcher? _____

11 How much do the bowl
and pitcher cost together? $_____

12 How much do the pitcher
and cup cost together? $_____

13 The pitcher and saucer cost $14.
How much does the saucer cost? $_____

NOTE TO HOME
Students solve word problems.

LESSON 22

Name _____

Using an Addition Table to Subtract

+	0	1	2	3	4	5	6	7	8	9	10
0	0	1	2	3	4	5	6	7	8	9	10
1	1	2	3	4	5	6	7	8	9	10	11
2	2	3	4	5	6	7	8	9	10	11	12
3	3	4	5	6	7	8	9	10	11	12	13
4	4	5	6	7	8	9	10	11	12	13	14
5	5	6	7	8	9	10	11	12	13	14	15
6	6	7	8	9	10	11	12	13	14	15	16
7	7	8	9	10	11	12	13	14	15	16	17
8	8	9	10	11	12	13	14	15	16	17	18
9	9	10	11	12	13	14	15	16	17	18	19
10	10	11	12	13	14	15	16	17	18	19	20

$17 - 9 = 8$

Find the answers in the addition table.

1. $17 - 8 =$ _____

2. $13 - 6 =$ _____

3. $6 - 4 =$ _____

4. $9 - 5 =$ _____

5. $15 - 5 =$ _____

6. $11 - 2 =$ _____

7. $9 - 3 =$ _____

8. $16 - 7 =$ _____

GAME

Play the "Roll 20 to 5" game.

NOTE TO HOME
Students learn how to use an addition table for subtraction.

◆ **LESSON 22 Using an Addition Table to Subtract**

Find the missing numbers.

9 8 + _____ = 17

10 11 – 3 = _____

11 8 + _____ = 11

12 11 – 8 = _____

13 17 – 8 = _____

14 17 – 9 = _____

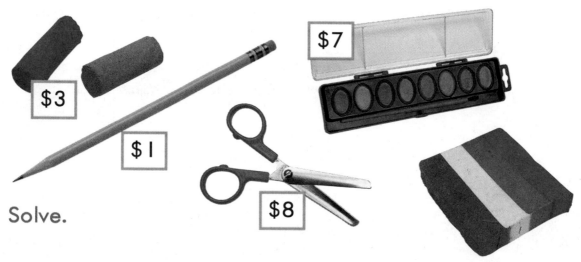

$3 $1 $8 $7

Solve.

15 If you have $15, can you buy
both the chalk and the paint set? _____

16 The paint set and scissors cost
$15 together. If you have $21,
how much money will you get back? $_____

17 Two packs of clay cost $12.
How much does one pack of clay cost? $_____

NOTE TO HOME
Students practice addition and subtraction
in number sentences and word problems.

Name _____

Adding and Subtracting

Check your math skills.

① 7 + 0 = _____   ② 2 + 7 = _____

③ 5 + 5 = _____   ④ 8 + 5 = _____

⑤ 6 + 5 = _____   ⑥ 1 + 7 = _____

⑦ 8 + 3 = _____   ⑧ 3 + 3 = _____

⑨ 4 + 6 = _____   ⑩ 8 + 2 = _____

⑪ 9 + 9 = _____   ⑫ 2 + 6 = _____

⑬ 8 + 10 = _____   ⑭ 9 + 7 = _____

⑮ 7 + 4 = _____   ⑯ 8 + 3 = _____

⑰ 5 + 9 = _____   ⑱ 7 + 5 = _____

⑲ 8 + 8 = _____   ⑳ 3 + 9 = _____

Number correct ▢

NOTE TO HOME
Students check their accuracy with addition facts.

◆ **LESSON 23   Adding and Subtracting**

Subtract.

㉑ 18 − 10 = _____   **㉒** 17 − 7 = _____

㉓ 13 − 10 = _____   **㉔** 14 − 4 = _____

㉕ 11 − 10 = _____   **㉖** 12 − 2 = _____

㉗ 16 − 9 = _____   **㉘** 16 − 7 = _____

㉙ 14 − 9 = _____   **㉚** 15 − 6 = _____

㉛ 18   **㉜** 15   **㉝** 13   **㉞** 19
    − 9   − 5   − 4   −10

㉟ 19   **㊱** 16   **㊲** 20
    − 9   − 6   −10

NOTE TO HOME
Students review subtraction facts
involving 9 and 10.

LESSON 24

Subtraction Facts

Subtract.

1 8 − 5 = _____   **2** 9 − 5 = _____

3 7 − 3 = _____   **4** 9 − 9 = _____

5 9 − 4 = _____   **6** 8 − 0 = _____

7 6 − 3 = _____   **8** 9 − 6 = _____

9
$$\begin{array}{r} 9 \\ -\ 3 \\ \hline \end{array}$$
10
$$\begin{array}{r} 9 \\ -\ 2 \\ \hline \end{array}$$
11
$$\begin{array}{r} 7 \\ -\ 4 \\ \hline \end{array}$$
12
$$\begin{array}{r} 5 \\ -\ 1 \\ \hline \end{array}$$
13
$$\begin{array}{r} 8 \\ -\ 3 \\ \hline \end{array}$$

14
$$\begin{array}{r} 7 \\ -\ 6 \\ \hline \end{array}$$
15
$$\begin{array}{r} 6 \\ -\ 1 \\ \hline \end{array}$$
16
$$\begin{array}{r} 9 \\ -\ 1 \\ \hline \end{array}$$
17
$$\begin{array}{r} 6 \\ -\ 0 \\ \hline \end{array}$$
18
$$\begin{array}{r} 5 \\ -\ 2 \\ \hline \end{array}$$

GAME

Play the "Space" game.

NOTE TO HOME
Students review and learn new subtraction facts.

◆ **LESSON 24 Subtraction Facts**

Subtract.

19 18 − 9 = _____

20 15 − 8 = _____

21 18 − 10 = _____

22 14 − 7 = _____

23 16 − 6 = _____

24 12 − 6 = _____

25 16 − 7 = _____

26 12 − 7 = _____

27 16 − 8 = _____

28 12 − 8 = _____

Solve.

29 Peggy has 12 marbles. If she loses
eight of them, how many will she have? _____

30 Carla had ten marbles. She won some more.
She has 15 marbles now. How many did she win? _____

31 Isaac has ten marbles. If he wins
seven more, how many will he have? _____

NOTE TO HOME
Students practice addition and
subtraction number sentences.

LESSON 25

Reviewing Subtraction Facts

Subtract.

1. $12 - 7 =$ _____

2. $12 - 5 =$ _____

3. $12 - 4 =$ _____

4. $11 - 4 =$ _____

5. $11 - 8 =$ _____

6. $10 - 3 =$ _____

7. $10 - 6 =$ _____

8. $12 - 10 =$ _____

9. $12 - 6 =$ _____

10. $10 - 10 =$ _____

11. $\begin{array}{r} 11 \\ -\ 9 \\ \hline \end{array}$
12. $\begin{array}{r} 11 \\ -\ 5 \\ \hline \end{array}$
13. $\begin{array}{r} 12 \\ -\ 8 \\ \hline \end{array}$
14. $\begin{array}{r} 10 \\ -\ 5 \\ \hline \end{array}$
15. $\begin{array}{r} 10 \\ -\ 4 \\ \hline \end{array}$

16. $\begin{array}{r} 11 \\ -\ 3 \\ \hline \end{array}$
17. $\begin{array}{r} 11 \\ -10 \\ \hline \end{array}$
18. $\begin{array}{r} 12 \\ -\ 1 \\ \hline \end{array}$
19. $\begin{array}{r} 11 \\ -\ 6 \\ \hline \end{array}$
20. $\begin{array}{r} 12 \\ -\ 2 \\ \hline \end{array}$

NOTE TO HOME
Students review subtraction facts.

◆ **LESSON 25** Reviewing Subtraction Facts

Subtract.

㉑ $11 - 7 =$ _____   ㉒ $11 - 1 =$ _____

㉓ $10 - 4 =$ _____   ㉔ $12 - 12 =$ _____

㉕ $10 - 7 =$ _____   ㉖ $11 - 0 =$ _____

㉗ $8 - 3 =$ _____   ㉘ $9 - 1 =$ _____

㉙ $9 - 0 =$ _____   ㉚ $8 - 7 =$ _____

| ㉛ $\begin{array}{r} 7 \\ -4 \\ \hline \end{array}$ | ㉜ $\begin{array}{r} 10 \\ -5 \\ \hline \end{array}$ | ㉝ $\begin{array}{r} 12 \\ -6 \\ \hline \end{array}$ | ㉞ $\begin{array}{r} 8 \\ -4 \\ \hline \end{array}$ | ㉟ $\begin{array}{r} 12 \\ -3 \\ \hline \end{array}$ |

| ㊱ $\begin{array}{r} 10 \\ -1 \\ \hline \end{array}$ | ㊲ $\begin{array}{r} 12 \\ -7 \\ \hline \end{array}$ | ㊳ $\begin{array}{r} 6 \\ -3 \\ \hline \end{array}$ | ㊴ $\begin{array}{r} 10 \\ -6 \\ \hline \end{array}$ | ㊵ $\begin{array}{r} 11 \\ -5 \\ \hline \end{array}$ |

NOTE TO HOME
Students practice and
review subtraction facts.

Name _____

Practicing Subtraction Facts

Subtract.

1 13 − 8 = _____   **2** 16 − 8 = _____

3 15 − 7 = _____   **4** 14 − 7 = _____

5 14 − 6 = _____   **6** 13 − 5 = _____

7 14 − 4 = _____   **8** 14 − 8 = _____

9 15 − 8 = _____   **10** 14 − 9 = _____

11 15 − 10 = _____   **12** 13 − 7 = _____

13 13 − 6 = _____   **14** 13 − 3 = _____

15 13 − 9 = _____   **16** 14 − 5 = _____

Play the "What's the Problem?" game.

NOTE TO HOME
Students practice subtraction facts including those
involving 13, 14, 15, and 16.

Unit 1   Lesson 26 • **55**

◆ **LESSON 26   Practicing Subtraction Facts**

Answer these questions.

⓱ I had $14. I bought a book. Now
I have $6. Which book did I buy? _____

⓲ I had $14. I bought a book. Now
I have $7. Which book did I buy? _____

_____

⓳ I had $14. I bought two books. I still
have $2. Which two books did I buy?

_____

_____

⓴ Can I buy the green and
blue books if I have $14? _____

㉑ Can I buy the green and
red books if I have $14? _____

NOTE TO HOME
Students solve money problems.

LESSON 27

Name _____

More Subtraction Practice

Subtract.

① $12 - 7 =$ _____

② $17 - 10 =$ _____

③ $14 - 7 =$ _____

④ $15 - 9 =$ _____

⑤ $13 - 8 =$ _____

⑥ $14 - 10 =$ _____

⑦ $10 - 6 =$ _____

⑧ $11 - 2 =$ _____

⑨ $9 - 2 =$ _____

⑩ $10 - 7 =$ _____

⑪ $\begin{array}{r} 6 \\ -1 \\ \hline \end{array}$

⑫ $\begin{array}{r} 8 \\ -4 \\ \hline \end{array}$

⑬ $\begin{array}{r} 5 \\ -3 \\ \hline \end{array}$

⑭ $\begin{array}{r} 11 \\ -5 \\ \hline \end{array}$

⑮ $\begin{array}{r} 18 \\ -8 \\ \hline \end{array}$

⑯ $\begin{array}{r} 7 \\ -6 \\ \hline \end{array}$

⑰ $\begin{array}{r} 18 \\ -9 \\ \hline \end{array}$

⑱ $\begin{array}{r} 4 \\ -4 \\ \hline \end{array}$

⑲ $\begin{array}{r} 16 \\ -7 \\ \hline \end{array}$

⑳ $\begin{array}{r} 11 \\ -6 \\ \hline \end{array}$

NOTE TO HOME
Students review all basic subtraction facts.

◆ **LESSON 27** **More Subtraction Practice**

Work these problems.

 $7

 $6

 $2

Kaya has $10.

㉑ Suppose she buys the ball.
How much change will she get? $_____

㉒ How much change if she buys the car? $_____

㉓ How much change if she buys the marbles? $_____

㉔ Does Kaya have enough money
to buy the ball and the car?   _____

㉕ Does she have enough money to
buy the ball and the marbles?   _____

THINKING STORY

Talk about the Thinking Story "Ferdie
Knows the Rules."

NOTE TO HOME
Students solve word problems.

LESSON 28

Subtraction Checkpoint

Check your math skills.

1. $20 - 10 =$ _____

2. $9 - 0 =$ _____

3. $17 - 9 =$ _____

4. $15 - 8 =$ _____

5. $16 - 7 =$ _____

6. $12 - 6 =$ _____

7. $14 - 4 =$ _____

8. $11 - 10 =$ _____

9. $8 - 1 =$ _____

10. $15 - 5 =$ _____

11. $18 - 9 =$ _____

12. $11 - 7 =$ _____

13. $16 - 8 =$ _____

14. $9 - 6 =$ _____

15. $13 - 10 =$ _____

16. $10 - 3 =$ _____

17. $12 - 8 =$ _____

18. $10 - 5 =$ _____

Number
correct

NOTE TO HOME
Students check their knowledge of
subtraction facts.

◆ **LESSON 28   Subtraction Checkpoint**

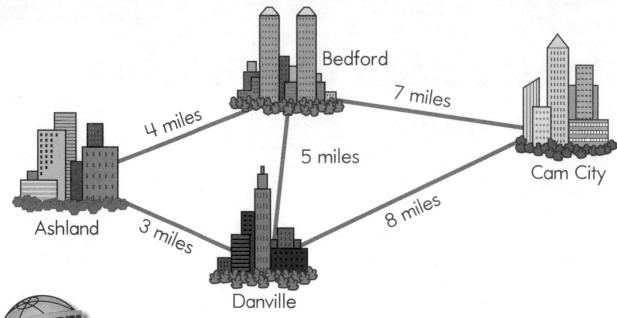

Use the map to answer the questions.

19 How far is it from Danville to Cam City?   _____

20 How much farther is it from Danville
to Cam City than from Danville to Bedford?   _____

21 Jill drove from Danville to
Cam City to Bedford. How far was that?   _____

22 Katie drove from Danville to
Ashland to Bedford. How far was that?   _____

23 Who drove farther?   _____

How much farther?   _____

24 Jason drove from Danville to Bedford directly.
How much farther did Jill drive than Jason?   _____

NOTE TO HOME
Students solve addition and subtraction word problems.

LESSON 29

Name _____

Using a Calculator

Using a calculator is easy.
Practice. Push the keys.
Look at the display.

1 + 8 = ?

Push [1]

Push [+]

Push [8]

Push [=]

What is your answer? _____

Push [C] to clear the display.

8 − 1 = ?

Push [8]

Push [−]

Push [1]

Push [=]

What is your answer? _____

Push [C] to clear the display.

Practice using your calculator.

① (4) (+) (8) (=) (___)   **②** 8 + 8 + 9 = _____

③ 4 + 7 = _____   **④** 3 + 6 + 5 = _____

⑤ 5 + 6 = _____   **⑥** 2 + 4 + 7 = _____

⑦ 8 − 7 = _____   **⑧** 16 − 9 = _____

 NOTE TO HOME
Students practice addition and subtraction
on a calculator.

◆ **LESSON 29   Using a Calculator**

Practice using your calculator. Work the problems. Then check them with a classmate.

Push **C** to clear the display after every problem.

9 [4] [+] [8] [=] [   ]

10 [9] [−] [6] [=] [   ]

11 [7] [+] [7] [=] [   ]

12 [1] [0] [−] [6] [=] [   ]

13 [1] [3] [−] [5] [=] [   ]

14 [2] [7] [−] [4] [=] [   ]

15 [2] [6] [+] [7] [=] [   ]

16 [6] [2] [+] [4] [=] [   ]

17 [1] [7] [+] [8] [=] [   ]

18 [1] [4] [+] [3] [+] [8] [=] [   ]

19 [2] [7] [−] [3] [−] [2] [=] [   ]

20 [4] [9] [−] [8] [−] [5] [=] [   ]

62 • Addition and Subtraction

NOTE TO HOME
Students practice using a calculator.

Name _____

Addition and Subtraction

Work these problems. Watch the signs.

1 8
   + 4

2 12
   − 8

3 4
   + 8

4 12
   − 4

5 9
   − 3

6 9
   + 9

7 8
   + 6

8 7
   − 4

9 14
   − 6

10 11
    − 3

11 8
    + 3

12 7
    + 4

13 6
    + 8

14 14
    − 7

15 11
    − 4

16 3
    + 8

17 6
    + 9

18 3
    + 7

NOTE TO HOME
Students practice addition and
subtraction facts mixed together.

Unit 1   Lesson 30 • **63**

◆ **LESSON 30** **Addition and Subtraction**

Solve these problems.

⑲ Mike has 20¢. A pencil costs 9¢.
Can Mike buy two pencils? _____
Can he buy three pencils? _____

⑳ Lisa had seven baseball cards.
She gave two of them away.
How many does she have now? _____

㉑ Paco has a $10 bill.
He buys a book for $4.
How much change
does he get? $ _____

㉒ Mrs. Simon has a $5 bill and a $10
bill. The hat she wants to buy costs
$12. Does she have enough money?

_____

NOTE TO HOME
Students solve word problems involving
addition and subtraction.

LESSON 31

Name _____

Applying Addition and Subtraction

Work these problems. Watch the signs.

①	8	②	8	③	14	④	20	⑤	13
	− 7		+ 7		− 5		−10		+ 5

⑥	6	⑦	0	⑧	17	⑨	8	⑩	9
	+ 7		+ 9		− 8		+ 4		− 3

⑪ 1 + 3 = _____   ⑫ 3 + 6 = _____

⑬ 13 − 4 = _____   ⑭ 10 + 5 = _____

⑮ 9 + 4 = _____   ⑯ 15 − 7 = _____

⑰ 14 − 9 = _____   ⑱ 12 − 8 = _____

NOTE TO HOME
Students practice addition and subtraction facts.

◆ **LESSON 31 Applying Addition and Subtraction**

Solve these problems.

⑲ Andrew had nine apples. He picked seven more apples. How many apples does he have now?

_____

⑳ Andrew used eight of the 16 apples to make a pie. How many apples does he have left?

_____

㉑ Suppose Andrew eats three of those apples. How many will be left? _____

㉒ If Andrew gives two of these apples to Brant and three to Brent, how many will be left?

_____

NOTE TO HOME
Students solve mixed word problems.

LESSON 32

Name _____

Adding and Subtracting Three Numbers

Work these problems. Watch the signs.

1 $5 + 5 + 4 =$ _____

Think:

$$\begin{array}{r} 5 \\ + 5 \end{array} \Big\} \; 10$$
$$+ \; 4 \Big\} \; 4$$
$$\overline{ 14}$$

2 $11 - 4 + 4 =$ _____

3 $10 - 8 + 7 =$ _____   4 $5 + 5 + 5 =$ _____

5 $4 + 8 - 2 =$ _____   6 $16 - 0 - 8 =$ _____

7
$$\begin{array}{r} 4 \\ 5 \\ + 9 \\ \hline \end{array}$$

8
$$\begin{array}{r} 8 \\ 2 \\ + 7 \\ \hline \end{array}$$

9
$$\begin{array}{r} 5 \\ 5 \\ + 5 \\ \hline \end{array}$$

10
$$\begin{array}{r} 7 \\ 3 \\ + 8 \\ \hline \end{array}$$

11
$$\begin{array}{r} 6 \\ 5 \\ + 8 \\ \hline \end{array}$$

12
$$\begin{array}{r} 6 \\ 3 \\ + 9 \\ \hline \end{array}$$

13
$$\begin{array}{r} 9 \\ 0 \\ + 5 \\ \hline \end{array}$$

14
$$\begin{array}{r} 4 \\ 5 \\ + 6 \\ \hline \end{array}$$

15
$$\begin{array}{r} 3 \\ 3 \\ + 3 \\ \hline \end{array}$$

16
$$\begin{array}{r} 2 \\ 7 \\ + 4 \\ \hline \end{array}$$

NOTE TO HOME
Students add and subtract three numbers.

◆ **LESSON 32** **Adding and Subtracting Three Numbers**

3¢ each

8¢ each

4¢ each

Solve these problems.

17 How much money for three crayons? _____¢

18 for two checkers and one crayon? _____¢

19 for four marbles? _____¢

20 for two crayons and one marble? _____¢

21 for one crayon, one checker, and one marble? _____¢

22 Jason has 15¢. Can he buy
two crayons and two marbles? _____

Play the "Roll a Number Sentence" game.

NOTE TO HOME
Students solve word problems.

LESSON 33

Name _____

Pictographs

Each figure stands for ten children.

Ms. Allen's class

Ms. Beck's class

Mr. Carl's class

Answer these questions.

① Which class has the least number of students? _____
How many? _____

② Which class has the greatest number of students? _____
How many? _____

③ How many children are in Mr. Carl's class? _____

④ How many more children are in
Mr. Carl's class than in Ms. Beck's class? _____

⑤ How many children are in Ms. Allen's
class and Ms. Beck's class all together? _____

⑥ Mr. Dixon's class has 20 children.
Draw a pictograph to show that.

NOTE TO HOME
Students read pictographs.

◆ **LESSON 33 Pictographs**

Each  stands for ten gallons of gas
used on a trip between two towns.

Albright to Trent

Albright to Wayne

Trent to Newtown

Newtown to Wayne

7 According to the pictograph, which two towns
are farthest apart? _____

8 According to the pictograph, which two towns
are the closest together? _____

9 How many gallons are used on
a trip from Trent to Newtown? _____

10 How many gallons are used on
a trip from Newtown to Wayne? _____

11 On a sheet of paper, draw a map that shows
where Albright, Trent, Wayne, and Newtown
might be. Compare your map with others.

NOTE TO HOME
Students read pictographs.

Name _____

Vertical Bar Graphs

Jenni, Ryan, Ladonna, Daniel, and Adam made a
bar graph showing how many books they read.

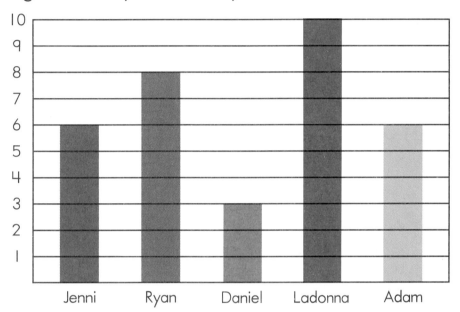

Jenni	Ryan	Daniel	Ladonna	Adam

Find the answers.

1 Who has read the most books? _____

How many? _____

2 Who has read the fewest books? _____

How many? _____

3 How many books has Jenni read? _____

4 How many books has Adam read? _____

5 How many books has Ryan read? _____

NOTE TO HOME
Students read vertical bar graphs.

◆ **LESSON 34 Vertical Bar Graphs**

Nora read seven books. Jordan read nine books.
Baxter has not read any books. Ian read five
books and Teresa read ten books.

Complete the bar graph.

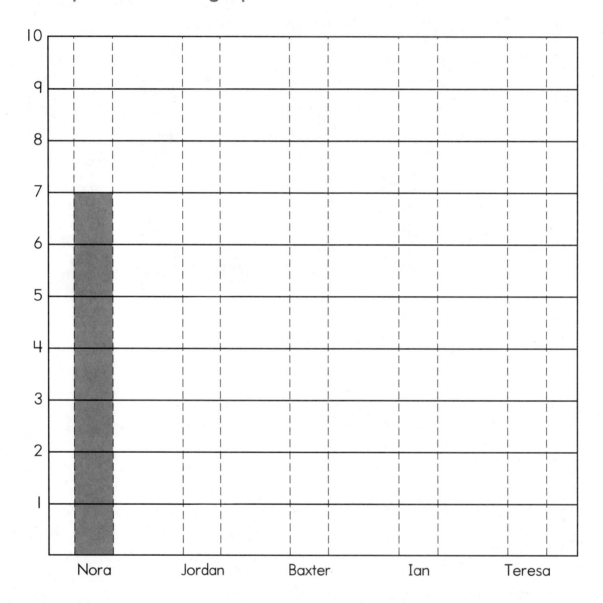

"The Tale of Peter Rabbit" by Beatrix Potter
is the best-selling children's book of all
time.

NOTE TO HOME
Students read vertical bar graphs.

LESSON
35

Name _____

Horizontal Bar Graphs

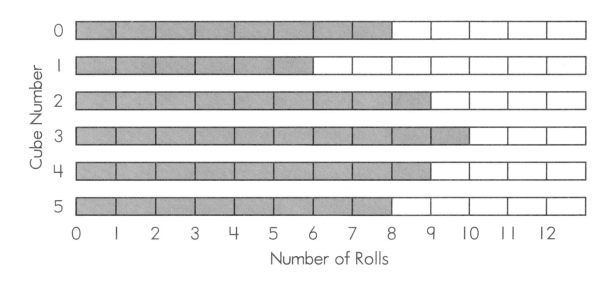

Cube Number

0
1
2
3
4
5

0 1 2 3 4 5 6 7 8 9 10 11 12

Number of Rolls

Ben is rolling a 0–5 cube. He is keeping records on the bar graph. He has rolled 50 times.

1 How many times has he rolled 0? _____

2 How many times has he rolled 1? _____

3 How many times has he rolled 2? _____

4 How many times has he rolled 3? _____

5 How many times has he rolled 4? _____

6 How many times has he rolled 5? _____

NOTE TO HOME
Students read horizontal bar graphs.

Unit 1   Lesson 35 • **73**

◆ **LESSON 35** Horizontal Bar Graphs

Work with another student.

Roll the 0–5 cube. Keep records on the bar graph. Stop when one number has been rolled ten times.

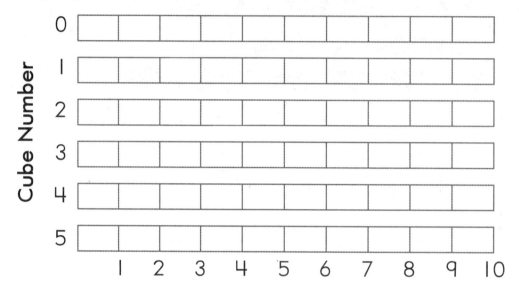

Roll a 5–10 cube. Keep records. Stop when a number has been rolled ten times.

NOTE TO HOME
Students record data on horizontal bar graphs.

74 • Addition and Subtraction

LESSON
36

Name _____

Place Value—Base Ten

How many sticks? Write your answers.

1

_36_

2

____

3

____

4

____

5

____

6

____

NOTE TO HOME
Students count tens and ones.

Unit 1   Lesson 36 • **75**

◆ **LESSON 36** Place Value—Base Ten

How much money? Write your answers.

7 _____ 32¢

8 _____

9 _____

10 _____

11 _____

THINKING STORY

Talk about the Thinking Story "Portia's Rules."

GAME

Play the "Get to 100 by Tens or Ones" game.

NOTE TO HOME
Students review counting money.

Name _____

Place Value—Using Money

Show each amount with coins. Draw as
few coins as you can.

1 37¢

2 65¢

3 82¢

4 17¢

5 34¢

NOTE TO HOME
Students show which coins make given
amounts of money.

◆ **LESSON 37** Place Value—Using Money

Draw coins to make 30¢. Try to do it with

6 2 coins

7 3 coins

8 4 coins

9 5 coins

10 6 coins

11 Can you do it with 7 coins? _____

NOTE TO HOME
Students show the same money
amount in different ways.

Name _____

Counting by Tens

Solve using mental math.

1 $10 + 0 =$ _____

2 $10 + 10 =$ _____

3 $10 + 10 + 10 =$ _____

4 $20 + 10 =$ _____

5 $10 + 10 + 10 + 10 =$ _____

6 $30 + 10 =$ _____

7 $10 + 10 + 10 + 10 + 10 =$ _____

8 $40 + 10 =$ _____

9 $10 + 10 + 10 + 10 + 10 + 10 =$ _____

10 $50 + 10 =$ _____

11 $10 + 10 + 10 + 10 + 10 + 10 + 10 =$ _____

12 $60 + 10 =$ _____

NOTE TO HOME
Students add tens.

◆ **LESSON 38** **Counting by Tens**

Work these problems. Watch the signs.

⑬   3 + 5 = _____   ⑭   30 + 50 = _____

⑮   5 + 2 = _____   ⑯   50 + 20 = _____

⑰   8 + 7 = _____   ⑱   80 + 70 = _____

⑲   9 – 3 = _____   ⑳   90 – 30 = _____

㉑   13 – 6 = _____   ㉒   130 – 60 = _____

㉓   8   ㉔   80   ㉕   7   ㉖   70
     + 4   + 40   – 3   – 30

Play the "Roll a Number" game.

Try to write this number—one centillion.
A centillion is 1 followed by 303 zeros.

NOTE TO HOME
Students add and subtract.

Name _____

Measuring Length— Centimeters

The centimeter is a unit of length.

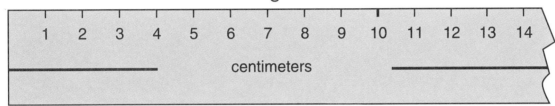

This pencil is 14 centimeters long.

This nail is 8 centimeters long.

How long are these? Use your centimeter ruler.
Write your answers.

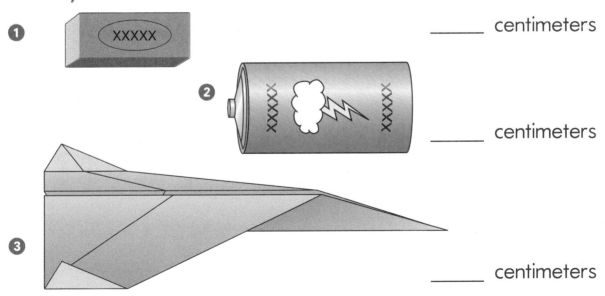

❶ _____ centimeters

❷ _____ centimeters

❸ _____ centimeters

NOTE TO HOME
Students use centimeter rulers to measure.

◆ **LESSON 39 Measuring Length—Centimeters**

Add the measures of the sides to find
the perimeter.

④

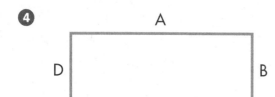

Side	Centimeters
A	
B	
C	
D	
Perimeter	

⑤

Side	Centimeters
A	
B	
C	
D	
Perimeter	

⑥

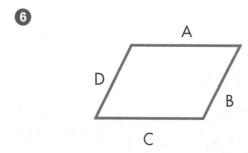

Side	Centimeters
A	
B	
C	
D	
Perimeter	

The world's longest bicycle held 35 people.
It was nearly 67 feet long.

NOTE TO HOME
Students measure perimeter.

LESSON
40

Name _____

Measurement—Meters and Centimeters

The meter and the centimeter are units of length.
There are 100 centimeters in 1 meter.

Meter can be
written as **m**

Centimeter can be
written as **cm**

| 1 cm | 10 | 20 | 30 | 40 | 50 | 60 | 70 | 80 | 90 | 100 |

 Do the "Measuring" activity.

Find three objects in the classroom that
are about 1 meter long. Write how many
centimeters long they are.

Object	Centimeters
❶ _____	_____
❷ _____	_____
❸ _____	_____

1 meter = 100 centimeters

❹ 2 m = _____ cm ❺ 4 m = _____ cm

❻ 3 m = _____ cm ❼ 6 m = _____ cm

 NOTE TO HOME
Students learn to measure in centimeters and meters.

◆ **LESSON 40   Measurement—Meters and Centimeters**

Measure.

Try to find something that is about 2 meters long or 2 meters high. Measure to see how many centimeters each is.

Object	Centimeters
8 _____	_____
9 _____	_____
10 _____	_____
11 _____	_____

Fill in the blanks.

12 7 m = _____ cm   **13** 10 m = _____ cm

14 _____ m = 500 cm   **15** _____ m = 400 cm

16 _____ m = 800 cm   **17** _____ m = 100 cm

18 _____ m = 900 cm   **19** _____ m = 600 cm

NOTE TO HOME
Students estimate and measure in centimeters.

LESSON
41

Name _____

Measuring Length—Inches

The inch is another unit of length.

This pencil is 5 inches long.

How long are these? Use an inch ruler.
Write your answers.

1  _____ inches

2  _____ inches

3  _____ inches

NOTE TO HOME
Students use an inch ruler to measure.

◆ **LESSON 41 Measuring Length—Inches**

A foot is 12 inches long.

Find some things in your classroom that are about a foot long. Measure them and tell how many inches long they are.

	Object	Inches
4	_____	_____
5	_____	_____
6	_____	_____
7	_____	_____

Find things that are about 2 feet long. Measure. How many inches long are they?

	Object	Inches
8	_____	_____
9	_____	_____

NOTE TO HOME
Students estimate and measure in inches.

LESSON 42

Name _____

Measurement—Yards, Feet, and Inches

The inch and the foot are units of length.
There are 12 inches in 1 foot.

The yard is also a unit of length. There are
3 feet or 36 inches in 1 yard.

Yard can be written as **yd**
Feet or foot can be written as **ft** and inches as **in**

How many? Use a ruler to count if you need to.

1 1 yard = _____ feet = _____ inches

2 2 yards = _____ feet = _____ inches

NOTE TO HOME
Students learn how to convert yards
and feet to inches.

◆ **LESSON 42** Measurement—Yards, Feet, and Inches

Find some things in your classroom that are about 1 yard long. Measure them. How many inches long are they?

Object   Inches

3 _____   _____

4 _____   _____

5 _____   _____

6 _____   _____

Complete the following. Use a ruler to count if you need to.

7 1 foot = 12 inches

8 _____ feet = 60 inches

9 _____ feet = 24 inches

10 _____ feet = 120 inches

11 4 feet = _____ inches

12 6 feet = _____ inches

Talk about the Thinking Story "Paint Up, Fix Up, Measure Up."

NOTE TO HOME
Students estimate and measure in yards, feet, and inches.

Name _____

Estimating Length

First estimate the length of each object in centimeters. Then measure to check. Write your answers.

❶ Estimate. about _____ cm

❷ Measure. _____ cm

❸ Estimate. about _____ cm

❹ Measure. _____ cm

❺ Estimate. about _____ cm

Measure. _____ cm

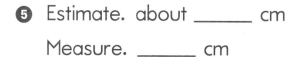

NOTE TO HOME
Students estimate how long, then measure to check their estimates.

◆ **LESSON 43 Estimating Length**

COOPERATIVE LEARNING   Do the "Measuring Length" activity.

6 How long?   Unit _____

Objects	Estimate Length	Measure Length	Difference

A kangaroo can leap over 25 feet in a single hop.

NOTE TO HOME
Students estimate length, measure objects, and record their findings.

LESSON
44

Name _____

Measurement– Perimeters

Find the perimeter.

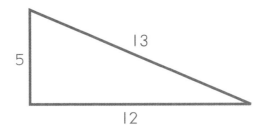

① perimeter = _____

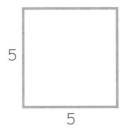

② perimeter = _____

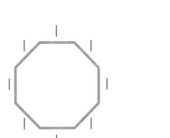

③ perimeter = _____

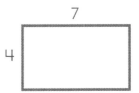

④ perimeter = _____

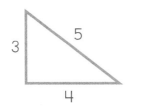

⑤ perimeter = _____

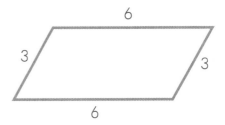

⑥ perimeter = _____

NOTE TO HOME
Students find the perimeter of figures.

◆ **LESSON 44** Measurement—Perimeters

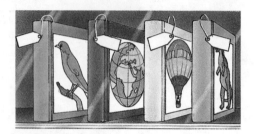 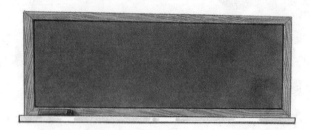

 Work with another student.

Measure some objects in your classroom, such
as your book, your chair, or a chalkboard.
Tell what the perimeter of each object is both
in centimeters and in inches.

Object	Perimeter in centimeters	Perimeter in inches
7 _____	_____	_____
8 _____	_____	_____
9 _____	_____	_____
10 _____	_____	_____
11 _____	_____	_____
12 _____	_____	_____

13 Which is greater, the number of inches in
the perimeter or the number of centimeters
in the perimeter? _____

14 Which is longer, an inch or a centimeter? _____

  NOTE TO HOME
Students measure objects and find
the perimeter.

Name _____

Unit 1 Test

Check your math skills. Count up or count down. Fill in the missing numbers.

1 | 4 | | | | 8 | 9 | | 11 |

2 | 36 | 37 | | | | | | 43 |

3 | 43 | 42 | | | | | | 36 |

4 | 21 | 20 | | | | | | 14 |

Work these problems. Watch the signs.

5   8 + 6 = _____   **6**   9 + 7 = _____

7   3 + 8 = _____   **8**   7 + 9 = _____

9   14 − 4 = _____   **10**   10 + 8 = _____

11 15   **12**   8   **13**   9   **14** 13
        − 7   + 8   + 3   − 4

NOTE TO HOME
This test checks unit skills and concepts.

◆ **LESSON 45 Unit 1 Test**

Solve these problems. Watch the signs.

⑮ 20 − 10 = _____   ⑯ 50 + 20 = _____

⑰ 30 + 40 = _____   ⑱ 80 − 50 = _____

⑲ 54 + 3 = _____   ⑳ 54 − 3 = _____

㉑ 65 − 3 = _____   ㉒ 76 + 3 = _____

㉓ 47 + 2 = _____   ㉔ 88 − 1 = _____

㉕ 66 + 1 = _____   ㉖ 51 + 2 = _____

㉗ 74 − 3 = _____   ㉘ 38 + 1 = _____

㉙
```
    8
    7
  + 3
  ___
```
㉚
```
    6
    4
  + 5
  ___
```
㉛
```
    4
    4
  + 4
  ___
```
㉜
```
    9
    0
  + 7
  ___
```

A skunk can spray you from ten feet away.

NOTE TO HOME
This test checks unit skills and concept.

◆ **LESSON 45 Unit 1 Test**

Name _____

How much money? Write your answers.

33   _____ ¢

34   _____ ¢

35    $_____

Solve these problems.

36 $3 + \boxed{} = 8$ **37** $5 + \boxed{} = 11$

38 $\boxed{} + 7 = 13$ **39** $\boxed{} + 8 = 16$

40 The toy train is _____ cm long.

NOTE TO HOME
This test checks unit skills and concept.

◆ **LESSON 45 Unit 1 Test**

Solve these problems.

41 Lonnie had seven strawberries. He picked five more. How many strawberries does he have now?_____

42 Eric has $15. He buys a hat for $6. How much money does he have left? $ _____

43 Theresa has 12¢. Stickers cost 5¢ each. Can Theresa buy two stickers? _____

44 Janell had 15 marbles. She lost some of them. How many does Janell have now? _____

45 Suzanne has five magazines. Her sister buys her two more. How many does Suzanne have now? _____

NOTE TO HOME
This test checks unit skills and concepts.

LESSON **46**

Name _____

Extending the Unit

 GAME

Play the "Dot-Square" game.

Game 1

Game 2

Game 3

Game 4

 NOTE TO HOME
Students play a game in which they try to make as many squares as possible.

Unit 1   Lesson 46 • **97**

◆ **LESSON 46 Extending the Unit**

Solve these problems.

1
```
    3
  + 4
  ───
```

2
```
   30
 + 40
 ────
```

3
```
    9
  − 5
  ───
```

4
```
   90
 − 50
 ────
```

5
```
    5
  + 4
  ───
```

6
```
   50
 + 40
 ────
```

7
```
   80
 − 30
 ────
```

8
```
   60
 + 30
 ────
```

9
```
   90
 − 10
 ────
```

10
```
    9
  − 9
  ───
```

11
```
   90
 − 90
 ────
```

12
```
   40
 + 20
 ────
```

13
```
    7
  + 4
  ───
```

14
```
   10
 + 40
 ────
```

15
```
   17
  − 9
 ────
```

16
```
   80
 − 70
 ────
```

17
```
    8
  + 7
  ───
```

18
```
   18
 + 70
 ────
```

19
```
   60
 + 6
 ────
```

20
```
   40
 + 12
 ────
```

NOTE TO HOME
Students add and subtract.

UNIT 2

Two-Digit Addition and Subtraction

RENAMING AND REGROUPING

- time
- fractions
- congruent figures
- symmetry
- money

Tile layers use math . . .

A tile layer covers floors, walls, or ceilings with tiles. Sometimes the tiles tessellate and sometimes they are the same size and shape. The tile layer must add up all of the measurements carefully to plan the design and to find out how many tiles will be needed to cover the area.

Name _____

Graphs

We use graphs to help record and organize information.

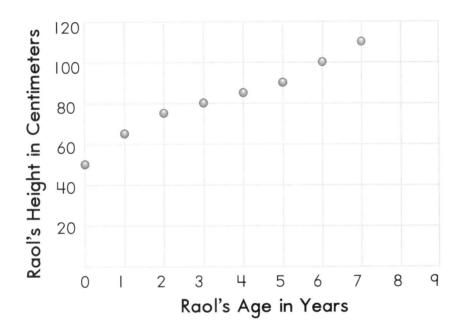

Use the graph to answer the questions.

1. How tall was Raol when he was three years old? _____ cm

2. About how old was Raol when he was 100 cm tall? _____

3. How tall was Raol when he was born? _____ cm

4. How tall was Raol when he was seven years old? _____ cm

NOTE TO HOME
Students read a graph.

◆ **LESSON 47 Graphs**

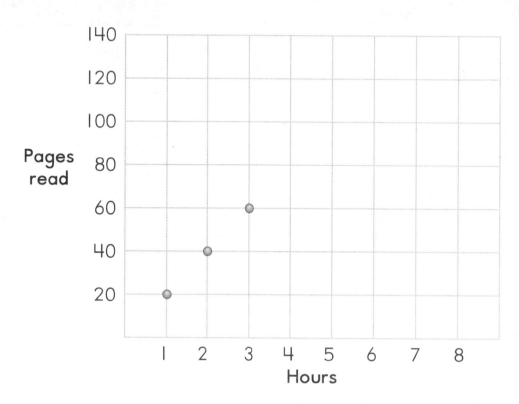

Use the graph to answer the questions.

Andrew is reading a book. After one hour, he had read 20 pages. He kept track on a graph.

❺ Do you see the point that shows one hour and 20 pages? Ring it.

❻ How many pages did he read in two hours?_____

❼ How many pages did he read in three hours?_____

❽ When do you think he will have read about 100 pages?_____

❾ Put a point on the graph for five hours and 100 pages.

❿ Put a point on the graph for four hours and the number of pages you think he might have read then.

NOTE TO HOME
Students read a grid and estimate.

LESSON
48

Name _____

Place Value

2 tens and 14 = 34

Use sticks to help.
Write the standard name for each of these.

1 5 tens and 7 = __57__

2 3 tens and 12 = __42__

3 2 tens and 8 = _____

4 2 tens and 13 = _____

5 4 tens and 18 = _____

6 8 tens and 0 = _____

7 6 tens and 8 = _____

8 5 tens and 10 = _____

9 8 tens and 19 = _____

10 0 tens and 8 = _____

11 1 ten and 8 = _____

12 1 ten and 14 = _____

13 0 tens and 17 = _____

14 3 tens and 15 = _____

15 7 tens and 16 = _____

16 4 tens and 18 = _____

NOTE TO HOME
Students use bundles of sticks to help
them write numbers in standard form.

◆ **LESSON 48   Place Value**

Each bundle has ten sticks. How many sticks in each picture?

17 _____

18 _____

19 _____

20 _____

21 _____

22 _____

23 _____

24 _____

25 _____

26 _____

NOTE TO HOME
Students count using groups of ten.

LESSON 49

Name _____

Adding Tens and Ones

Use sticks or other objects to solve these problems.

 +

1   50 sticks   +   23 sticks   =   _____ sticks

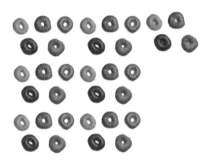 +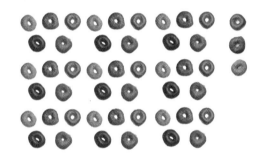

2   34 bagels   +   48 bagels   =   _____ bagels

 +

3   28 peanuts   +   24 peanuts   =   _____ peanuts

NOTE TO HOME
Students use models to help them add tens and ones.

◆ **LESSON 49 Adding Tens and Ones**

How much?

4 34¢ + 22¢ = _____ ¢

5 51¢ + 16¢ = _____ ¢

Use sticks or other objects to solve these problems.

6 17 + 18 = _____

7 26 + 37 = _____

8 82 + 17 = _____

9 13 + 68 = _____

10 26 + 37 = _____

11 53 + 42 = _____

12 16 + 69 = _____

13 41 + 28 = _____

14 23 + 15 = _____

15 39 + 13 = _____

16 39 + 14 = _____

17 13 + 21 = _____

18 46 + 22 = _____

19 11 + 45 = _____

NOTE TO HOME
Students continue using models to help them add tens and ones.

LESSON 50

Name _____

Adding Two-Digit Numbers

Use sticks or other objects to solve these problems.

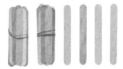

1 46 sticks + 24 sticks = _____ sticks

2 23 dollars + 21 dollars = _____ dollars

3 23¢ + 15¢ = _____ ¢

Play the "Make 10 Bingo" game.

NOTE TO HOME
Students add two-digit numbers whose sums are multiples of ten.

◆ **LESSON 50** **Adding Two-Digit Numbers**

Use sticks to add.

31 + 19 = _____

Write what you did.

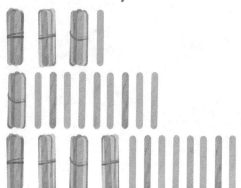

3 tens   and 1

+ 1 ten   and 9

4 tens   and 10

or

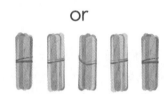

or

5 tens   and 0

④   14   1 ten   and 4
   + 36   +3 tens and 6
             _____ tens and _____   or _____ tens and _____

⑤   17   1 ten   and 7
   + 13   +1 ten   and 3
             _____ tens and _____   or _____ tens and _____

NOTE TO HOME
Students continue using models to
understand adding two-digit numbers.

LESSON 51

Name _____

Two-Digit Numbers

Use sticks to add.

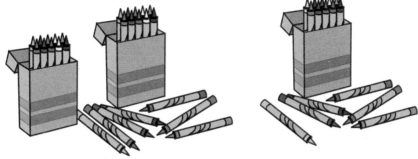

1 27 crayons + 16 crayons = _____ crayons

2 40 checkers + 32 checkers = _____ checkers

3 35 paper clips + 35 paper clips = _____ paper clips

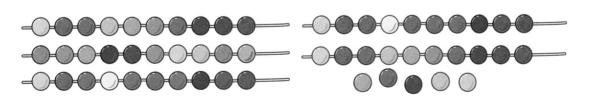

4 30 beads + 25 beads = _____ beads

NOTE TO HOME
Students practice solving problems
by adding two-digit numbers.

Unit 2   Lesson 51 • **109**

◆ LESSON 51   Two-Digit Numbers

Use sticks to add.

28 + 35 = ____

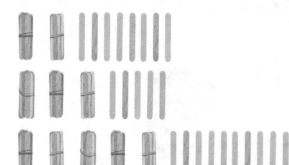

2 tens and 8

+ 3 tens and 5
_____

5 tens and 13

or   or

6 tens and 3

Write what you did.

5   27   2 tens   and 7
    + 36   + 3 tens   and 6
    _____

    ____ tens   and ____   or ____ tens and ____

6   44   4 tens   and 4
    + 56   + 5 tens   and 6
    _____

    ____ tens   and ____   or ____ tens and ____

Play the "Get to 100 with the 5–10 Cube" game.

Talk about the Thinking Story "Ferdie's Meterstick."

NOTE TO HOME
Students practice and play a game where they must add two-digit numbers.

Name _____

Adding with Renaming

Add.

$$34 + 58 = \underline{\quad ? \quad}$$

3 tens and 4

+ 5 tens and 8

34

+ 58

I ten
3 tens and 4

+ 5 tens and 8
          2

I
34

+ 58
     2

I ten
3 tens and 4

+ 5 tens and 8

9 tens and 2

I
34

+ 58
    92

NOTE TO HOME
Students learn a standard procedure for
adding two-digit numbers.

◆ **LESSON 52 Adding with Renaming**

Add. Write your answers.

①
```
  1
  89
+  7
―――
  96
```

②
```
  19
+ 46
```

③
```
  15
+ 15
```

④
```
  25
+ 25
```

⑤
```
  45
+ 45
```

⑥
```
  94
+  6
```

⑦
```
   0
+ 73
```

⑧
```
  30
+ 57
```

⑨
```
  89
+  1
```

⑩
```
  89
+ 10
```

⑪
```
  27
+ 36
```

⑫
```
  24
+ 55
```

⑬
```
  36
+  6
```

⑭
```
  36
+ 16
```

⑮
```
  59
+  9
```

⑯
```
  59
+ 29
```

Did you know that it takes nearly two days for your body to digest a meal?

NOTE TO HOME
Students solve addition problems with regrouping.

Name _____

Two-Digit Addition

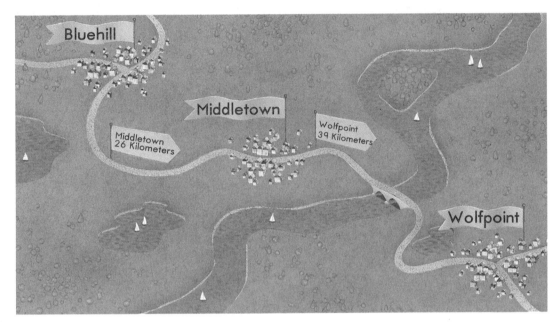

Use the map to answer the questions.

① How far is it from Bluehill to Middletown
to Wolfpoint?

_____ kilometers + _____ kilometers = _____ kilometers

② How far is it from Wolfpoint to Middletown
to Bluehill?

_____ kilometers + _____ kilometers = _____ kilometers

③ How far is it from Bluehill to Middletown
and back to Bluehill?

_____ kilometers + _____ kilometers = _____ kilometers

NOTE TO HOME
Students solve word problems.

Unit 2   Lesson 53 • **113**

◆ **LESSON 53 Two-Digit Addition**

29¢

63¢

45¢

Solve the problems.

❹ How much do the pen
and pencil cost together? _____ ¢

❺ How much do the toy soldier
and balloon cost together? _____ ¢

❻ How much do the doll
and pen cost together? _____ ¢

❼ How much do two pens cost? _____ ¢

❽ How much do two pencils cost? _____ ¢

❾ How much do two toy soldiers cost? _____ ¢

❿ I have one dollar (100 cents). Can I
buy the toy soldier and the doll? _____

⓫ What is the greatest number of
different things I can buy for one dollar? _____

48¢

12¢

NOTE TO HOME
Students solve word problems.

LESSON 54

Name _____

More Two-Digit Addition

Add. Write the answers.

1
$$\begin{array}{r} 78 \\ +\ 1 \\ \hline 79 \end{array}$$

2
$$\begin{array}{r} 78 \\ +10 \\ \hline \end{array}$$

3
$$\begin{array}{r} 43 \\ +\ 7 \\ \hline \end{array}$$

4
$$\begin{array}{r} 43 \\ +17 \\ \hline \end{array}$$

5
$$\begin{array}{r} 62 \\ +21 \\ \hline \end{array}$$

6
$$\begin{array}{r} 34 \\ +46 \\ \hline \end{array}$$

7
$$\begin{array}{r} 34 \\ +47 \\ \hline \end{array}$$

8
$$\begin{array}{r} 62 \\ +20 \\ \hline \end{array}$$

9
$$\begin{array}{r} 28 \\ +17 \\ \hline \end{array}$$

10
$$\begin{array}{r} 63 \\ +37 \\ \hline \end{array}$$

11
$$\begin{array}{r} 22 \\ +44 \\ \hline \end{array}$$

12
$$\begin{array}{r} 39 \\ +18 \\ \hline \end{array}$$

13
$$\begin{array}{r} 25 \\ +25 \\ \hline \end{array}$$

14
$$\begin{array}{r} 39 \\ +49 \\ \hline \end{array}$$

15
$$\begin{array}{r} 43 \\ +21 \\ \hline \end{array}$$

16
$$\begin{array}{r} 43 \\ +11 \\ \hline \end{array}$$

17
$$\begin{array}{r} 40 \\ +37 \\ \hline \end{array}$$

18
$$\begin{array}{r} 53 \\ +21 \\ \hline \end{array}$$

19
$$\begin{array}{r} 53 \\ +20 \\ \hline \end{array}$$

20
$$\begin{array}{r} 42 \\ +36 \\ \hline \end{array}$$

NOTE TO HOME
Students practice adding two-digit numbers
with and without regrouping.

◆ **LESSON 54   More Two-Digit Addition**

Solve the problems.

Bus Schedule			
From Granville	Leaves	Arrives	Round Trip Price
to Allentown	2:17 PM	8:32 PM	$32
to Choirville	6:54 AM	11:43 AM	$24
to Middlebury	7:02 AM	4:38 PM	$48
to Park City	11:50 AM	1:20 PM	$9
to Danville	12:43 PM	9:47 PM	$53

㉑ How much will it cost to take trips
to both Park City and Allentown? $_____

㉒ How much will it cost to take trips
to both Middlebury and Allentown? $_____

㉓ How much will it cost to take trips
to both Danville and Choirville? $_____

㉔ What time does the bus leave for Middlebury?

_____

Which city do you think is closest to Granville?
Explain your answer in your Math Journal.

NOTE TO HOME
Students practice addition and
reading a table.

LESSON
55

Name _____

Practicing Two-Digit Addition

How well can you add? Write the answers.

1　56
　　+ 28

2　34
　　+ 27

3　28
　　+ 41

4　25
　　+ 25

5　34
　　+ 55

6　61
　　+ 29

7　37
　　+ 58

8　43
　　+ 7

9　75
　　+ 19

10　82
　　+ 7

11　　8
　　+ 49

12　28
　　+ 27

13　26
　　+ 54

14　28
　　+ 25

15　43
　　+ 26

16　35
　　+ 44

17　52
　　+ 21

18　63
　　+ 18

19　49
　　+ 20

20　44
　　+ 44

Number correct ▢

NOTE TO HOME
Students check their skill with two-digit addition.

◆ **LESSON 55** Practicing Two-Digit Addition

Players throw darts. If the sum equals 96, the player wins a teddy bear.

96 WINS!

㉑ Which pair of numbers totals 96? _____

㉒ Can you make 96 by adding three of the numbers? _____

㉓ If so, which three? _____

㉔ Are there other ways to make 96 by using some numbers more than once?

_____

 **NOTE TO HOME**
Students solve two-digit word problems.

Name _____

Keeping Sharp

Check your math skills.

1   8
  – 5

2   10
  – 4

3   13
  – 7

4   16
  – 6

5   12
  – 7

6   14
  – 9

7   15
  – 8

8   18
  – 10

9   7
  – 3

10   10
  – 6

11   17
  – 8

12   16
  – 8

13   15
  – 9

14   14
  – 8

15   13
  – 5

16   9
  – 3

17   14
  – 7

18   12
  – 6

19   14
  – 4

20   6
  – 2

Number correct [ ]

NOTE TO HOME
Students check their subtraction skills.

◆ **LESSON 56 Keeping Sharp**

Solve these problems.

21 Rosa had $17.

She spent $9.

How much money does she have now? $_____

22 Sam had 30 pennies.

He traded them for dimes.

How many dimes did he get? _____

23 Petra planted ten bean seeds.

Eight of them sprouted.

How many didn't sprout? _____

24 Casey had 29 soda cans.

She collected 18 more.

How many did she have together? _____

NOTE TO HOME
Students solve word problems.

LESSON
57

Name _____

Renaming Tens as Ones

Rewrite to show one fewer ten.

55 = 4 tens and 15

1 63 = _____ tens and _____

2 49 = _____ tens and _____

3 38 = _____ tens and _____

NOTE TO HOME
Students begin learning how to rewrite
numbers for subtraction.

◆ **LESSON 57** **Renaming Tens as Ones**

Rewrite each number to show one fewer ten.

4 43 = __3__ tens and __13__

5 60 = 5 tens and ____

6 22 = 1 ten and ____

7 100 = ____ tens and ____

8 36 = ____ tens and ____

9 89 = ____ tens and ____

10 15 = ____ tens and ____

11 56 = ____ tens and ____

12 78 = ____ tens and ____

13 97 = ____ tens and ____

14 46 = ____ tens and ____

15 61 = ____ tens and ——

16 50 = ____ tens and ____

17 14 = ____ tens and ____

18 48 = ____ tens and ____

19 37 = ____ tens and ____

NOTE TO HOME
Students practice rewriting numbers for subtraction.

122 • Two-Digit Addition and Subtraction

LESSON
58

Name _____

Subtracting Multiples of Ten

Solve these problems.

1 Mika had 80¢.
She spent 50¢. Now she has _____ ¢.

2 Jerry has 50¢.
The cherries cost 80¢. He needs _____ ¢.

3 30 − 10 = _____

4 80 − 20 = _____

NOTE TO HOME
Students subtract multiples of ten.

◆ **LESSON 58** Subtracting Multiples of Ten

Use sticks or other objects to subtract.

5
$$\begin{array}{r} 60 \\ -30 \\ \hline \end{array}$$

6
$$\begin{array}{r} 80 \\ -40 \\ \hline \end{array}$$

7
$$\begin{array}{r} 100 \\ -50 \\ \hline \end{array}$$

8
$$\begin{array}{r} 70 \\ -20 \\ \hline \end{array}$$

9
$$\begin{array}{r} 100 \\ -30 \\ \hline \end{array}$$

10
$$\begin{array}{r} 40 \\ -0 \\ \hline \end{array}$$

11
$$\begin{array}{r} 20 \\ -10 \\ \hline \end{array}$$

12
$$\begin{array}{r} 60 \\ -10 \\ \hline \end{array}$$

13
$$\begin{array}{r} 90 \\ -20 \\ \hline \end{array}$$

14
$$\begin{array}{r} 80 \\ -70 \\ \hline \end{array}$$

15
$$\begin{array}{r} 80 \\ -10 \\ \hline \end{array}$$

16
$$\begin{array}{r} 50 \\ -30 \\ \hline \end{array}$$

17
$$\begin{array}{r} 80 \\ -20 \\ \hline \end{array}$$

18
$$\begin{array}{r} 30 \\ -30 \\ \hline \end{array}$$

19
$$\begin{array}{r} 20 \\ -10 \\ \hline \end{array}$$

20
$$\begin{array}{r} 80 \\ -30 \\ \hline \end{array}$$

21
$$\begin{array}{r} 50 \\ -10 \\ \hline \end{array}$$

22
$$\begin{array}{r} 40 \\ -10 \\ \hline \end{array}$$

23
$$\begin{array}{r} 70 \\ -0 \\ \hline \end{array}$$

24
$$\begin{array}{r} 10 \\ -0 \\ \hline \end{array}$$

GAME

Play the "Add or Subtract a Ten" game.

NOTE TO HOME
Students subtract multiples of ten.

LESSON
59

Name _____

Subtracting Two-Digit Numbers from Multiples of Ten

$$60 - 37 = \underline{\quad ? \quad}$$

I can't take 7 from 0.

$$\begin{array}{r} 60 \\ -\ 37 \\ \hline \end{array}$$ 6 tens and 0
− 3 tens and 7

I can undo a bundle of ten.

$$\begin{array}{cc} 5 & 10 \\ \not6 & \not0 \\ -\ 3 & 7 \\ \hline \end{array}$$ 5   10
$\not6$ tens and $\not0$
− 3 tens and 7

Now I can take 3 tens and 7.

$$\begin{array}{cc} 5 & 10 \\ \not6 & \not0 \\ -\ 3 & 7 \\ \hline 2 & 3 \end{array}$$ 5   10
$\not6$ tens and $\not0$
− 3 tens and 7
2 tens and 3

NOTE TO HOME
Students use sticks to model subtraction of two-digit numbers.

◆ LESSON 59 Subtracting Two-Digit Numbers from Multiples of Ten

Subtract. Use sticks to help. Record what you did.

1 90 − 48 = ___?___

	8 10	8 10
9 tens and 0	9̷ tens and 0̷	90
− 4 tens and 8	− 4 tens and 8	− 48

2 100 − 54 = ___?___

	9 10	9 10
10 tens and 0	1̷0̷ tens and 0̷	100
− 5 tens and 4	− 5 tens and 4	− 54

3 80 − 30 =   _____ tens and _____   80

− _____ tens and _____   − 30

4 70 − 48 =   _____ tens and _____   70

− _____ tens and _____   − 48

126 • Two-Digit Addition and Subtraction

NOTE TO HOME
Students subtract with regrouping.

LESSON 60

Name _____

Two-Digit Subtraction

Solve these problems.

| ① 40 −27 | ② 100 −93 | ③ 74 −13 | ④ 55 −10 |

| ⑤ 60 −28 | ⑥ 70 −19 | ⑦ 36 −27 | ⑧ 84 −26 |

⑨ Michael had 80¢.
He spent 46¢.

He has _____ ¢ left.

⑩ Yoshie had 50¢.
She spent 25¢.

She has _____ ¢ left.

⑪ Ashley had 90¢.
She spent 50¢.

She has _____ ¢ left.

⑫ Debra had 46¢.
She spent 25¢.

She has _____ ¢ left.

⑬ Ivan had 40¢.
He spent 37¢.

He has _____ ¢ left.

⑭ Rob had 75¢.
He spent 39¢.

He has _____ ¢ left.

THINKING STORY

Talk about the Thinking Story
"How Far Up? How Far Down?"

NOTE TO HOME
Students work subtraction and word problems.

Unit 2   Lesson 60 • **127**

GAME

◆ **LESSON 60** Two-Digit Subtraction

Three-Cube Subtraction

Players: Two or more

Materials: One 0–5 cube, one 0–5 tens cube, and one 5–10 tens cube and paper and pencil

RULES

Leader: Roll all three cubes and make a two-digit number from the numbers shown on the 0–5 cube and the 0–5 tens cube. Subtract the number shown on the 5–10 tens cube.

Players: Each of the other players does the same thing.

Winner: The person who has the greatest difference wins the round.

I played the game with

_____

NOTE TO HOME
Students subtract two-digit numbers.

LESSON 61

Name _____

Subtracting Two-Digit Numbers

Subtract. Use sticks to help.

53 − 25 = ___?___

I can't take 5 from 3.

53   5 tens and ③
− 25 − 2 tens and ⑤

If I undo a bundle of 10, I have 13

4 13   4   13
5̶ 3̶   5̶ tens and 3̶
− 2 5 − 2 tens and 5

4 13
5̶ 3̶   5̶ tens and 3̶
− 2 5 − 2 tens and 5
        2 tens and 8

NOTE TO HOME
Students subtract two-digit numbers.

◆ **LESSON 61** Subtracting Two-Digit Numbers

Subtract. Use sticks to help.
Record what you did.

❶ 22 – 13 = ?

_____ tens and _____   22
– _____ tens and _____   – 13

❷ 50 – 25 = ?

_____ tens and _____   50
– _____ tens and _____   – 25

❸ 44 – 29 = ?

_____ tens and _____   44
– _____ tens and _____   – 29

❹   83
        – 73

❺   100
        – 25

❻   17
        – 17

❼   49
        – 29

❽   27
        – 13

❾   63
        – 37

❿   18
        – 9

⓫   36
        – 18

NOTE TO HOME
Students practice subtraction with
two-digit numbers.

Name _____

Practicing Two-Digit Subtraction

Remember.

$$\begin{array}{r} 83 \\ -25 \\ \hline \end{array} \qquad \begin{array}{r} {\scriptstyle 7\ \ 13} \\ \cancel{8}\ \cancel{3} \\ -2\ 5 \\ \hline \end{array} \qquad \begin{array}{r} {\scriptstyle 7\ \ 13} \\ \cancel{8}\ \cancel{3} \\ -2\ 5 \\ \hline 5\ 8 \end{array}$$

Subtract. Write your answers.

1 $\begin{array}{r} 70 \\ -43 \\ \hline \end{array}$ **2** $\begin{array}{r} 72 \\ -43 \\ \hline \end{array}$ **3** $\begin{array}{r} 74 \\ -43 \\ \hline \end{array}$ **4** $\begin{array}{r} 68 \\ -39 \\ \hline \end{array}$

5 $\begin{array}{r} 81 \\ -26 \\ \hline \end{array}$ **6** $\begin{array}{r} 47 \\ -23 \\ \hline \end{array}$ **7** $\begin{array}{r} 45 \\ -25 \\ \hline \end{array}$ **8** $\begin{array}{r} 33 \\ -17 \\ \hline \end{array}$

9 $\begin{array}{r} 64 \\ -17 \\ \hline \end{array}$ **10** $\begin{array}{r} 38 \\ -35 \\ \hline \end{array}$ **11** $\begin{array}{r} 41 \\ -20 \\ \hline \end{array}$ **12** $\begin{array}{r} 46 \\ -29 \\ \hline \end{array}$

NOTE TO HOME
Students practice subtraction of two-digit numbers.

◆ **LESSON 62** Practicing Two-Digit Subtraction

Solve these problems.

⓫ David had 63¢. He spent 28¢.

Now he has _____ ¢.

⓮ Yori has 43¢. She needs 62¢.

She needs _____ ¢ more.

⓯ Jacob has 43¢. Emily has 39¢.

Who has more? _____

How much more? _____ ¢

⓰ Lani has 78¢. Tina has 92¢.

Who has more? _____

How much more? _____ ¢

Play the "Four-Cube Subtraction" game.

NOTE TO HOME
Students solve word problems and play
a subtraction game.

Name _____

Applying Subtraction

Solve these problems.

① 73
    − 48

② 63
    − 37

③ 52
    − 22

④ 49
    − 27

⑤ 50
    − 25

⑥ 66
    − 57

⑦ 88
    − 44

⑧ 32
    − 18

⑨ This chair was 94 cm high.
Matt cut 4 cm off each leg.

Now how high is the chair? _____ cm

⑩ Beth is 93 cm tall. Her brother
Daniel is 86 cm tall.

Who is taller? _____

How much taller? _____ cm

NOTE TO HOME
Students solve subtraction and word problems.

Unit 2   Lesson 63 • **133**

◆ **LESSON 63** **Applying Subtraction**

Solve these problems.

⓫ Natalie had $76. She bought shoes.
She now has $_____.

⓬ Rachel bought a shirt. She gave the clerk two
$20 bills. How much change did she get? $_____

⓭ Simon has $90. He wants to buy a jacket
and slacks. Can he? _____

⓮ Stan has a $50 bill. He buys slacks and a belt.
How much change should he get? $_____

⓯ Tyrone bought a shirt, slacks, and a belt.
He gave the clerk four $20 bills. How much
change should he get? $_____

NOTE TO HOME
Students solve word problems
involving money.

LESSON
64

Name _____

Subtracting with Money

Marta has $50. Enrique has $32.

1 Can Enrique buy the bicycle? _____

2 Could Marta and Enrique
buy the bicycle together? _____

3 If Marta and Enrique buy the bicycle
together, how much money will they have left? $ _____

4 If Marta buys the kite, how much
money will she have left? $ _____

5 If Enrique buys the baseball and bat,
how much money will he have left? $ _____

NOTE TO HOME
Students solve word problems involving money.

◆ **LESSON 64 Subtracting with Money**

Lisa said "I have 90¢."

Martin said "I have 95¢."

Look at the picture. Make up some problems. Then solve them.

_____

_____

_____

_____

_____

NOTE TO HOME
Students make up and solve
word problems.

Name _____

Checking Subtraction

Ring each wrong answer.

(Six of the answers are wrong.)

1
```
   17
 −  8
    9
```

2
```
   84
 − 27
   57
```

3
```
   61
 − 34
   26
```

4
```
   70
 − 43
   27
```

5
```
   29
 − 23
   52
```

6
```
   40
 − 32
   18
```

7
```
  100
 − 70
   30
```

8
```
   45
 − 25
   18
```

9
```
   64
 − 35
   38
```

10
```
   75
 − 25
   50
```

11
```
   85
 − 73
   12
```

12
```
   83
 − 25
   58
```

13
```
   87
 − 38
   49
```

14
```
   76
 − 35
   35
```

15
```
   92
 − 13
   79
```

16
```
   70
 − 43
   27
```

NOTE TO HOME
Students check answers to subtraction problems.

◆ **LESSON 65 Checking Subtraction**

Solve these problems.

17 Arnold bought film for 12 pictures.
He has already taken three pictures.
How many more can he take? _____

18 Toothpaste costs 84¢.
The toothbrush costs 79¢.
Which costs more? _____
How much more? _____ ¢

19 Rosa has 95¢. Janet has 59¢.
Who has more? _____
How much more? _____ ¢

20 Sara had 73 football cards.
She gave some away.
Now she has 45 cards.
How many did she give away? _____

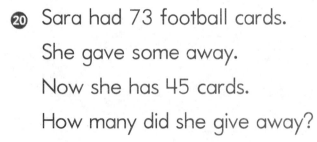

NOTE TO HOME
Students solve subtraction
word problems.

LESSON
66

Name _____

Subtraction Check

How well can you subtract? Write your answers.

1   56
   −29

2   83
   −27

3   46
   −23

4   38
   −35

5   84
   −30

6   27
   −19

7   75
   −25

8   26
   − 7

9   64
   −38

10   50
   −35

11   46
   − 8

12   63
   −17

13   97
   −34

14   61
   −56

15   74
   −42

16   86
   −29

Number correct [   ]

NOTE TO HOME
Students show their mastery of two-digit subtraction.

◆ **LESSON 66** **Subtraction Check**

17 Mitsu is 93 cm tall. David is 78 cm tall.

Who is taller? _____

How much taller? _____ cm

18 Aaron weighs 76 pounds. Paige weighs 54 pounds.

Who is heavier? _____

How much heavier? _____ pounds

19 Rob can run 300 yards in 57 seconds. Clarence can run 300 yards in 48 seconds.

Who is faster? _____

How much faster? _____ seconds

20 Mr. Han is 73 years old. Ms. Clay is 48 years old.

Who is older? _____

How much older? _____ years

21 Dani is 15 years old.

How much older is Mr. Han than Dani? _____ years

22 How much older is Ms. Clay than Dani? _____ years

NOTE TO HOME
Students solve word problems.

LESSON 67

Name _____

Addition and Subtraction

Solve these problems. Watch the signs.

①
```
  87
- 43
```

②
```
  66
+ 33
```

③
```
  66
- 33
```

④
```
  81
- 39
```

⑤
```
  50
+ 25
```

⑥
```
  50
- 25
```

⑦
```
  64
+ 27
```

⑧
```
  18
+ 18
```

⑨
```
  41
- 23
```

⑩
```
  56
- 36
```

⑪
```
  37
+ 29
```

⑫
```
  47
- 23
```

⑬
```
  51
+ 26
```

⑭
```
  27
+ 29
```

⑮
```
  43
- 28
```

GAME

Play the "Roll a Problem" game.

NOTE TO HOME
Students practice and play a game to review
addition and subtraction.

Unit 2   Lesson 67 • **141**

◆ **LESSON 67   Addition and Subtraction**

16 Mr. Moe lives 64 miles from Malltown.

Ms. Harris lives 37 miles from Malltown.

Who lives farther from Malltown? _____

How much farther? _____ miles

17 Ms. Ali lives at 83 Malvista Drive.

Ms. Hamad lives at 98 Malvista Drive.

How far apart are their houses? _____

Mr. Moe weighs 82 kilograms.
Mr. Harris weighs 54 kilograms.
Ms. Ali weighs 49 kg.
Ms. Hamad weighs 73 kg.

18 How much more does
Mr. Moe weigh than Ms. Ali? _____ kg

19 How much more does
Mr. Moe weigh than Ms. Hamad? _____ kg

20 How much more does
Ms. Hamad weigh than Ms. Ali? _____ kg

21 How much more does
Mr. Harris weigh than Ms. Ali? _____ kg

NOTE TO HOME
Students practice word problems.

LESSON **68**

Name _____

Practice Adding and Subtracting

Solve these problems. Watch the signs.

1 43
  + 25

2 37
  − 36

3 64
  − 38

4 18
  + 47

5 Jessica has 19¢.
If she earns 75¢,
how much will she have? _____¢

6 There are 27 children in the class.
Each child needs two pencils.
How many pencils are needed? _____

7 Kareem had 37¢.
He spent 15¢.
Now he has _____¢.

8 Cindy has 82¢.
If she spends 16¢,
how much will she have? _____¢

NOTE TO HOME
Students practice solving word problems.

◆ **LESSON 68** **Practice Adding and Subtracting**

Solve these problems.

9 Mr. Lin has $90.

Can he buy the
jacket and pants? _____

Can he buy the
jacket and hat? _____

Can he buy the
pants and hat? _____

10 There are 17 children in the library.
Each child has two books.

How many books
do they have all together? _____

11 There are 25 dogs in
Mr. Breezy's training
school. Each dog has
one tail.

How many tails do
they have all together? _____

Talk about the Thinking Story "Plenty of Time."

NOTE TO HOME
Students solve word problems.

UNIT 2

Name _____

Mid-Unit Review

Write the standard name for each of these.

1 4 tens and 9 = _____   **2** 6 tens and 0 = _____

3 5 tens and 16 = _____   **4** 0 tens and 19 = _____

Add.

5 $\begin{array}{r} 37 \\ +\ 6 \\ \hline \end{array}$ **6** $\begin{array}{r} 16 \\ +25 \\ \hline \end{array}$ **7** $\begin{array}{r} 75 \\ +20 \\ \hline \end{array}$ **8** $\begin{array}{r} 28 \\ +48 \\ \hline \end{array}$

9 $\begin{array}{r} 59 \\ +21 \\ \hline \end{array}$ **10** $\begin{array}{r} 0 \\ +47 \\ \hline \end{array}$ **11** $\begin{array}{r} 63 \\ +24 \\ \hline \end{array}$ **12** $\begin{array}{r} 35 \\ +\ 9 \\ \hline \end{array}$

Solve this problem.

13 Bob has 32 toy cars. His brother has 29 toy cars. How many cars do they have together? _____

Subtract.

14 $\begin{array}{r} 40 \\ -10 \\ \hline \end{array}$ **15** $\begin{array}{r} 80 \\ -30 \\ \hline \end{array}$ **16** $\begin{array}{r} 90 \\ -42 \\ \hline \end{array}$ **17** $\begin{array}{r} 100 \\ -67 \\ \hline \end{array}$

18 $\begin{array}{r} 82 \\ -37 \\ \hline \end{array}$ **19** $\begin{array}{r} 75 \\ -45 \\ \hline \end{array}$ **20** $\begin{array}{r} 54 \\ -22 \\ \hline \end{array}$ **21** $\begin{array}{r} 68 \\ -53 \\ \hline \end{array}$

NOTE TO HOME
Students review unit skills and concepts.

◆ UNIT 2 Mid-Unit Review

Solve these problems.

22 May had 65¢. She spent 25¢.
How much does she have now? _____ ¢

23 Jose needs $72. He has $46.
How much more does he need? $_____

Work these problems. Watch the signs.

24
$$42 \\ -\ 27$$

25
$$56 \\ +\ 24$$

26
$$39 \\ +\ 30$$

27
$$83 \\ -\ 78$$

28
$$79 \\ -\ 15$$

29
$$51 \\ +\ 44$$

30
$$93 \\ -\ 66$$

31
$$48 \\ +\ 36$$

32 $18 - 11 =$ _____

33 $21 - 11 =$ _____

Solve these problems.

34 Janell has 25 blue cars and
36 red cars.
How many more red cars
than blue cars does she have? _____

35 Elissa got $25 for her birthday. She
earned $7 more raking leaves.
How much did she have all together? $_____

NOTE TO HOME
Students review unit skills and concepts.

LESSON
69

Name _____

Check Your Adding and Subtracting

Solve these problems. Watch the signs.

1   53
    + 28

2   53
    − 28

3   47
    − 24

4   66
    + 27

5   36
    + 22

6   83
    − 39

7   44
    + 39

8   17
    + 59

98¢

Aaron has 27¢. Tanya has 35¢.

9   Who has more money? _____

10 How much more? _____ ¢

11 Together, how much
    do Tanya and Aaron have? _____ ¢

29¢

12 How much more does the
    comic book cost than the pen? _____ ¢

NOTE TO HOME
Students solve addition and subtraction problems.

◆ **LESSON 69 Check Your Adding and Subtracting**

Solve these problems.

⑬ This corn plant is
81 centimeters tall.
One week ago it was
69 centimeters tall.
How much did it grow last week? _____ cm

⑭ Juan has a $10 bill.
How much change will he
get if he buys the globe? $_____

$6

⑮ How much for two oranges? _____¢

⑯ How much for one
orange and one apple? _____¢

oranges
39¢ each

apples
10¢ each

⑰ Anita needs 75¢.
She already has 50¢.
How much more does she need? _____¢

How are adding and subtracting
alike and different? Write about
it in your Math Journal.

NOTE TO HOME
Students solve word problems.

Telling Time— Hour and Half Hour

What time is it? Write your answers.

7 o'clock or 7:00   30 minutes after 7 o'clock or 7:30

1    8 : 30

2    ___ : ___

3    ___ : ___

4 ___ : ___

5   ___ : ___

6    ___ : ___

7    ___ : ___

8 ___ : ___

NOTE TO HOME
Students review telling time to the nearest half hour.

Show the time.

9 4:00

10 10:30

11 1:30

12 6:00

13 7:30

14 three-thirty

15 five o'clock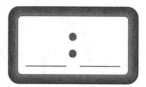

 Play the "Time" game.

NOTE TO HOME
Students review time and play a game
involving telling time.

LESSON 71

Name _____

Telling Time— Quarter Hour

What time is it?

 15 minutes after 7 o'clock
or quarter after 7 o'clock

 15 minutes before 8 o'clock
or quarter to 8 o'clock

1  quarter after ____

half past ____

quarter to ____

____ o'clock

2 quarter after ____

half past ____

quarter to ____

____ o'clock

3 `3:30` quarter after ____

half past ____

quarter to ____

____ o'clock

4 quarter after ____

half past ____

quarter to ____

____ o'clock

5  quarter after ____

half past ____

quarter to ____

____ o'clock

6 `12:00` quarter after ____

half past ____

quarter to ____

____ o'clock

 NOTE TO HOME
Students tell time to the quarter hour.

What time is it?

7 quarter after _____
half past _____
quarter to _____
_____ o'clock

8 quarter after _____
half past _____
quarter to _____
_____ o'clock

9 quarter after _____
half past _____
quarter to _____
_____ o'clock

10 quarter after _____
half past _____
quarter to _____
_____ o'clock

11 quarter after _____
half past
quarter to _____
_____ o'clock

12 quarter after _____
half past _____
quarter to _____
_____ o'clock

13 `10:30` quarter after _____
half past _____
quarter to _____
_____ o'clock

14 quarter after _____
half past _____
quarter to _____
_____ o'clock

 No wonder we get tired of left over turkey! Americans eat 50 million (50,000,000) turkeys on Thanksgiving.

 NOTE TO HOME
Students practice telling time to the quarter hour.

◆ LESSON 71 Telling Time—Quarter Hour

Name _____

What time is it?

15 _____ : _____

16 _____ : _____

17 _____ : _____

18 _____ : _____

19 _____ : _____

20 _____ : _____

21 _____ : _____

22 _____ : _____

NOTE TO HOME
Students tell time.

◆ LESSON 71 Telling Time—Quarter Hour

Sharpen your skills.

Solve these problems. Watch the signs.

㉓
```
   34
 + 34
```

㉔
```
   34
 - 34
```

㉕
```
   83
 - 17
```

㉖
```
   52
 - 27
```

㉗
```
   83
 + 17
```

㉘
```
   67
 - 37
```

㉙
```
   42
 + 56
```

㉚
```
   60
 - 43
```

㉛
```
   29
 + 53
```

㉜
```
   66
 - 38
```

㉝
```
   24
 - 17
```

㉞
```
   84
 - 20
```

㉟
```
   39
 - 18
```

㊱
```
   65
 - 49
```

㊲
```
   43
 + 16
```

㊳
```
   52
 + 24
```

㊴
```
   76
 - 35
```

㊵
```
   14
 + 77
```

NOTE TO HOME
Students review adding and subtracting
two-digit numbers.

LESSON
72

Name _____

Telling Time—Halves and Quarters

What time is it?

①  ____ : ____

② 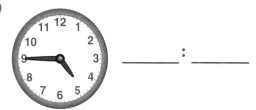 ____ : ____

③ 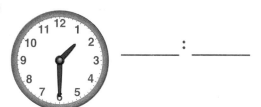 ____ : ____

④  ____ : ____

⑤  ____ : ____

⑥  ____ : ____

⑦  ____ : ____

⑧ 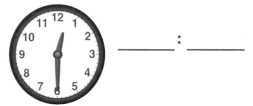 ____ : ____

⑨  ____ : ____

⑩  ____ : ____

NOTE TO HOME
Students learn to tell time to the half and quarter hour.

◆ **LESSON 72** Telling Time—Halves and Quarters

Draw the hands to show the time.

11   2:30

12   2:45

13   3:00

14   5:15

15   7:00

16   7:45

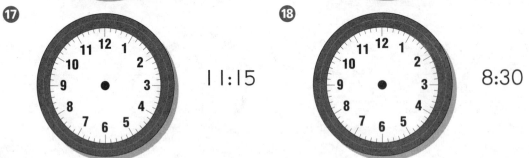

17   11:15

18   8:30

Play the "Harder Time" game.

NOTE TO HOME
Students show time on a clock and play a game.

LESSON
73

Name _____

Fractions—Halves and Quarters

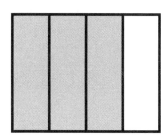

Three quarters of this rectangle is shaded.

Color one half $\left(\frac{1}{2}\right)$.

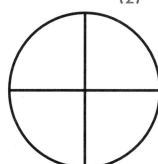

Color one quarter $\left(\frac{1}{4}\right)$.

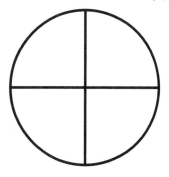

Color two quarters $\left(\frac{2}{4}\right)$.

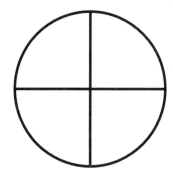

Color three quarters $\left(\frac{3}{4}\right)$.

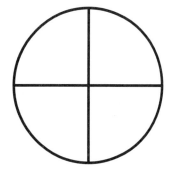

THINKING STORY

Talk about the Thinking Story "Take a Chance."

NOTE TO HOME
Students identify halves and quarters.

◆ **LESSON 73 Fractions—Halves and Quarters**

Solve these problems.

❶ Lani has a quarter (25¢).
   Kevin has a quarter (25¢).
   How much money
   do they have all together? _____

❷ Mel has a quarter (25¢).
   Carla has a quarter (25¢).
   How much money
   do they have all together? _____

❸ How much money do Lani, Kevin,
   Mel, and Carla have all together? _____

Watch the signs.

❹	❺	❻	❼	❽
64 + 23	75 − 63	87 + 12	87 + 13	29 + 37

❾	❿	⓫	⓬	⓭
46 − 37	50 − 25	50 + 25	75 + 25	18 + 63

NOTE TO HOME
Students review adding and subtracting
two-digit numbers.

LESSON 74

Name _____

Halves, Quarters, and Thirds

Color one half ($\frac{1}{2}$) of each figure.

1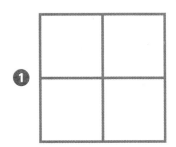

2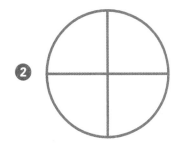

Color one quarter (one fourth or $\frac{1}{4}$) of each figure.

3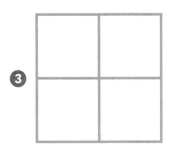

4

Color two quarters (two fourths or $\frac{2}{4}$) of each figure.

5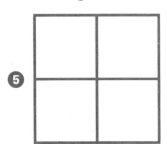

6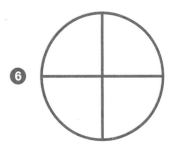

7 How many quarters in one half ($\frac{1}{2}$)? _____

NOTE TO HOME
Students practice identifying fractional parts ($\frac{1}{2}$, $\frac{1}{4}$, and $\frac{2}{4}$).

◆ **LESSON 74** **Halves, Quarters, and Thirds**

Color one third $\left(\frac{1}{3}\right)$ of each figure.

8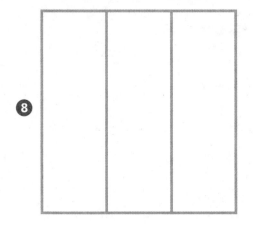

9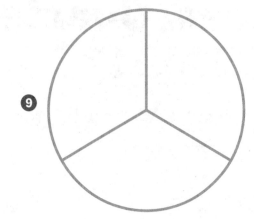

Color two thirds $\left(\frac{2}{3}\right)$ of each figure.

10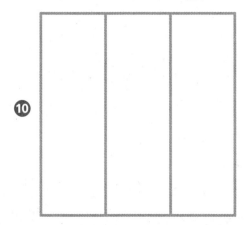

11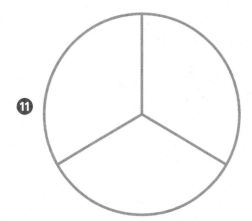

Color three quarters $\left(\frac{3}{4}\right)$ of each figure.

12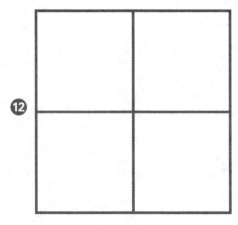

13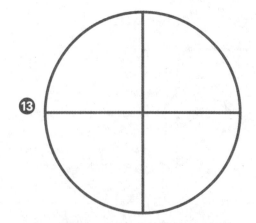

NOTE TO HOME
Students identify fractional
parts ($\frac{1}{3}$, $\frac{2}{3}$, and $\frac{3}{4}$).

◆ **LESSON 74** Halves, Quarters, and Thirds

Name _____

Color one quarter $\left(\frac{1}{4}\right)$ four different ways.

14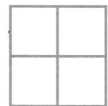

Color two thirds $\left(\frac{2}{3}\right)$ three different ways.

15

Color two quarters $\left(\frac{2}{4}\right)$ six different ways.

16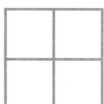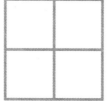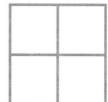

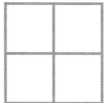 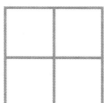 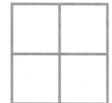

NOTE TO HOME
Students color fractional parts ($\frac{1}{4}$, $\frac{2}{3}$, and $\frac{2}{4}$) different ways.

◆ **LESSON 74** **Halves, Quarters, and Thirds**

Color $\frac{2}{3}$ in three different ways.

17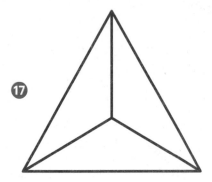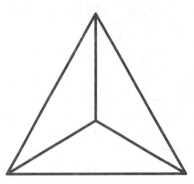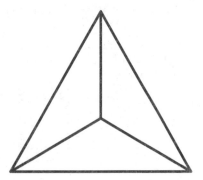

Color $\frac{2}{5}$ in six different ways.

18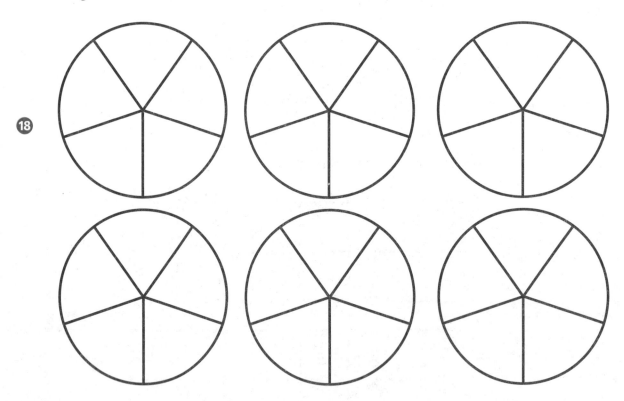

You can tell how old a fish is by counting the rings on its scales.

 NOTE TO HOME
Students color fractional parts.

LESSON 75

Name _____

Fifths and Other Fractions

Color one fifth $\left(\frac{1}{5}\right)$.

1

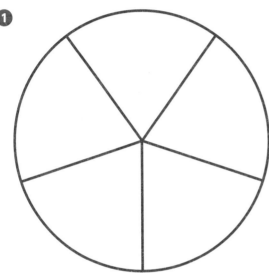

Color three fifths $\left(\frac{3}{5}\right)$.

2

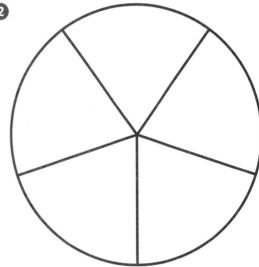

Color two fifths $\left(\frac{2}{5}\right)$.

3

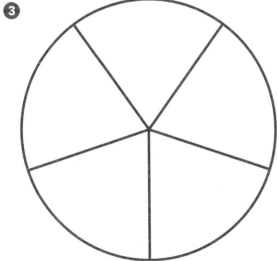

Color four fifths $\left(\frac{4}{5}\right)$.

4

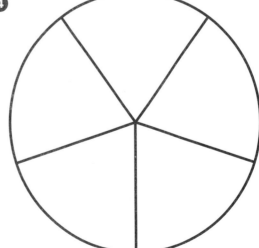

NOTE TO HOME
Students identify fractional parts (fifths).

◆ **LESSON 75** **Fifths and Other Fractions**

Color four fifths $\left(\frac{4}{5}\right)$.

5

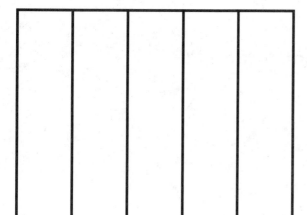

Color three fifths $\left(\frac{3}{5}\right)$.

6

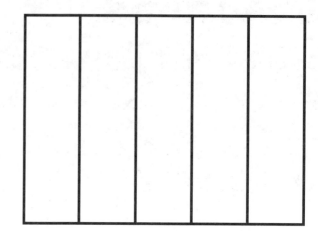

Color two fifths $\left(\frac{2}{5}\right)$.

7

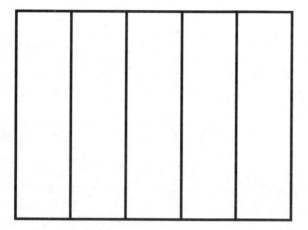

Color one fifth $\left(\frac{1}{5}\right)$.

8

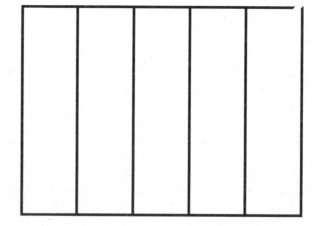

NOTE TO HOME
Students identify fractional parts
(fifths).

164 • Two-Digit Addition and Subtraction

◆ **LESSON 75** **Fifths and Other Fractions**

Name _____

Ring each wrong answer.
(Eight of the answers are wrong.)

⑨ 18 − 7 = __10__

⑩ 14 − 7 = __8__

⑪ 17 − 7 = __10__

⑫ 7 − 7 = __15__

⑬ 16 − 9 = __7__

⑭ 13 − 8 = __5__

⑮ 16 − 10 = __6__

⑯ 15 − 9 = __8__

⑰ 15 − 5 = __10__

⑱ 15 − 7 = __7__

⑲ 12 − 9 = __4__

⑳ 14 − 9 = __5__

㉑ 11 − 7 = __5__

㉒ 14 − 6 = __7__

㉓ 12 − 6 = __6__

NOTE TO HOME
Students identify incorrect answers to
subtraction problems.

Unit 2   Lesson 75 • **165**

◆ **LESSON 75 Fifths and Other Fractions**

Play the "Fraction" game.

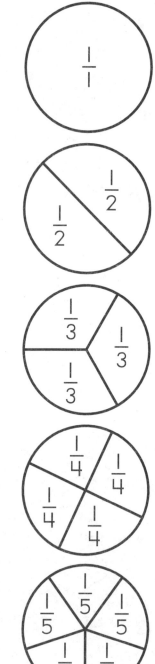

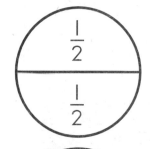

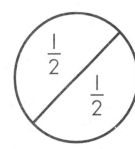

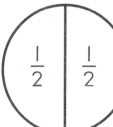

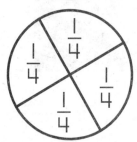

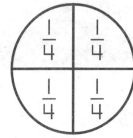

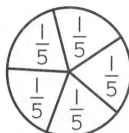

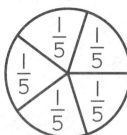

NOTE TO HOME
Students play a game in which they identify fractional parts.

LESSON 76

Name _____

Fractions and Geometry

Color one quarter $\left(\frac{1}{4}\right)$.

Color two quarters $\left(\frac{2}{4}\right)$.

1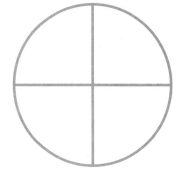

2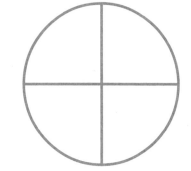

Color three quarters $\left(\frac{3}{4}\right)$.

Color four quarters $\left(\frac{4}{4}\right)$.

3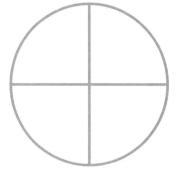

4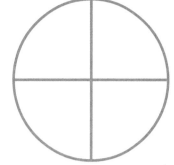

Color one quarter $\left(\frac{1}{4}\right)$ of the clock face.

Color one half $\left(\frac{1}{2}\right)$ of the clock face.

5

6

NOTE TO HOME
Students practice identifying fractional parts.

Unit 2   Lesson 76 • **167**

◆ **LESSON 76**   **Fractions and Geometry**

Make a dot where you think the center of
the clock is. Then cut out the clock. Fold it
in half. Then fold it in quarters. Was your
dot in the center of the clock?

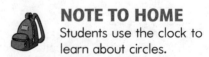

NOTE TO HOME
Students use the clock to
learn about circles.

Fractions

Name _____

What fraction is shaded?

1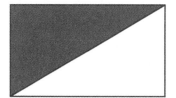

_____

2

_____

3

_____

4

_____

5

_____

6

_____

7

_____

8

_____

9

_____

NOTE TO HOME
Students identify fractional parts.

◆ **LESSON 77** **Fractions**

What fraction is shaded?

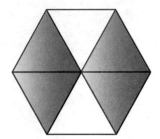

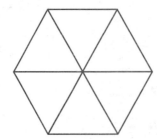

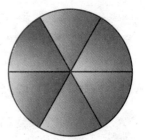

10 _____

11 _____

12 _____

What fraction of each of the following sets has a ring around it?

13 _____

14 _____

15 _____

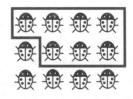

16 _____

17 _____

18 _____

Talk about the Thinking Story "Half a Job."

170 • Two-Digit Addition and Subtraction

NOTE TO HOME
Students identify fractional parts.

LESSON 78

Name _____

Fractions of Numbers

Complete the chart. Use your play coins
to help you.

	Make this amount.	Use this kind of coin.		How many coins?
1	$1		nickel	
2	$1		quarter	
3	$1		dime	
4	50¢		quarter	
5	50¢		dime	
6	50¢		nickel	

7 How much is $\frac{1}{4}$ of $1? _____ ¢

8 How much is $\frac{1}{2}$ of $1? _____ ¢

NOTE TO HOME
Students use coins to make different money amounts.

◆ **LESSON 78** **Fractions of Numbers**

Find the answers. You may use sticks or other objects to help.

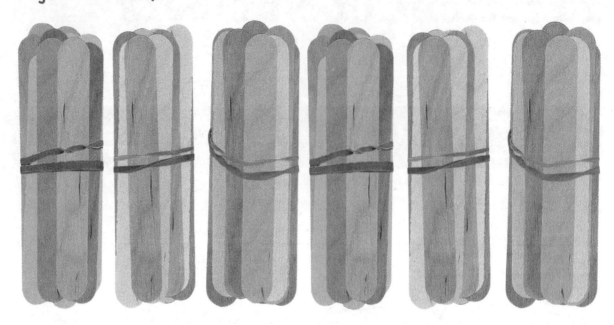

9 $\frac{1}{4}$ of 60 = _____

10 $\frac{2}{4}$ of 60 = _____

11 $\frac{3}{4}$ of 60 = _____

12 $\frac{4}{4}$ of 60 = _____

13 $\frac{1}{2}$ of 60 = _____

14 $\frac{2}{2}$ of 60 = _____

15 $\frac{1}{2}$ of 100 = _____

16 $\frac{2}{2}$ of 100 = _____

NOTE TO HOME
Students solve fraction of number problems.

LESSON
79

Name _____

Geometric Shapes–
Plane Figures

COOPERATIVE LEARNING Work with a partner.

right triangle

parallelogram

rectangle

1 Cut to make two right triangles.

2 Cut to make two rectangles.

3 Cut to make two parallelograms.

4 Cut differently to make two parallelograms.

5 Cut to make two triangles.

6 Cut differently to make two triangles.

NOTE TO HOME
Students review properties of two-dimensional figures.

◆ **LESSON 79** Geometric Shapes—Plane Figures

7 Cut to make two right triangles.

8 Cut to make four squares.

9 Cut to make one right triangle and one triangle that is not a right triangle.

10 Cut to make two triangles that are not right triangles.

11 Cut to make two pieces from which you can make a rectangle.

12 Cut to make two rectangles that are not squares.

NOTE TO HOME
Students review two-dimensional figures.

LESSON 80

Name _____

Congruent Shapes

Which are the same shape and same size?
Match the figures.

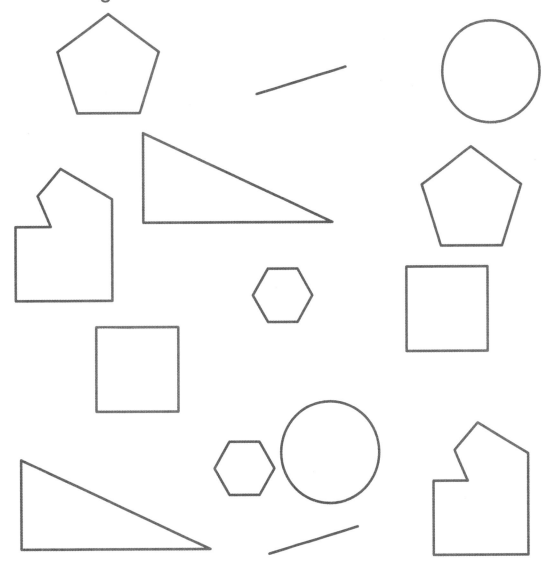

Talk about your answers. Trace to check.

NOTE TO HOME
Students identify congruent (same shape and same
size) shapes.

Unit 2   Lesson 80 • **175**

Copyright © SRA/McGraw-Hill

◆ **LESSON 80** **Congruent Shapes**

Which are the same shape and same size?

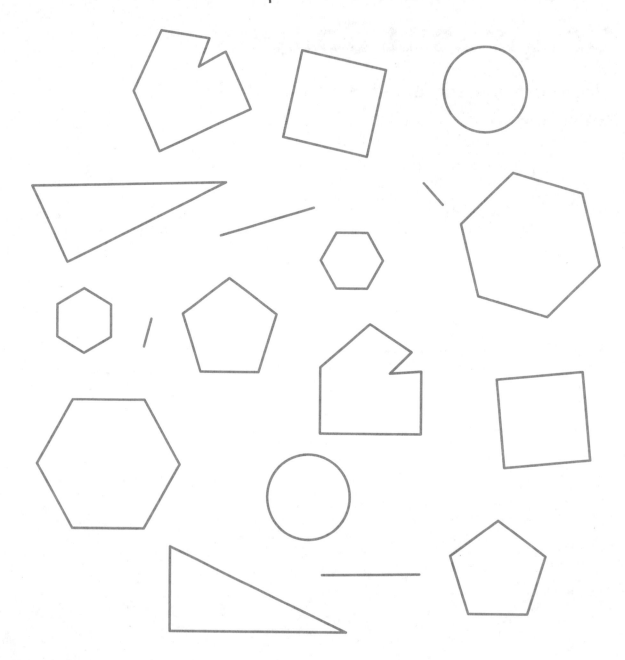

List some times we have to have congruent shapes. Tell why they are important.

NOTE TO HOME
Students identify congruent shapes.

LESSON 81

Name _____

Symmetry

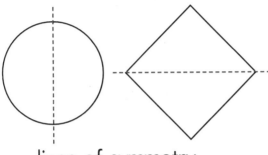

lines of symmetry

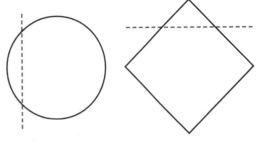

not lines of symmetry

Draw as many lines of symmetry as you can.

1

2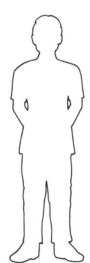

3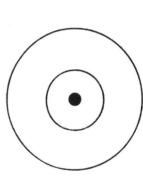

4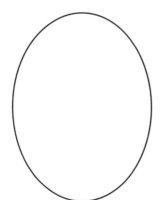

5

6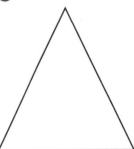

NOTE TO HOME
Students demonstrate their understanding of symmetry
by drawing lines of symmetry.

◆ **LESSON 81** **Symmetry**

Draw as many lines of symmetry as you can.

7. A   8. B   9. C   10. D

11. E   12. F   13. G   14. H

15. I   16. J   17. K   18. L

19. M   20. N   21. O   22. P

23. Q   24. R   25. S   26. T

27. U   28. V   29. W   30. X

31. Y   32. Z

NOTE TO HOME
Students draw lines of symmetry through
as many letters as they can.

LESSON
82

Name _____

Geometric Shapes—Solid Figures

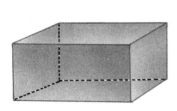

prism

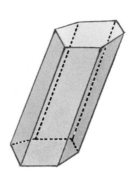

prism

prism

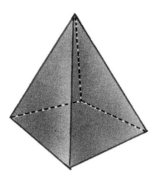

pyramid

pyramid

sphere

cone

cylinder

NOTE TO HOME
Students are introduced to solid figures.

◆ **LESSON 82   Geometric Shapes—Solid Figures**

❶ Name at least four objects that are prisms.

_____

_____

❷ Name four spheres.

_____

_____

❸ Name two cones and two cylinders.

_____

_____

_____

_____

 China is so big that it covers 6 time zones.

NOTE TO HOME
Students identify solid figures.

LESSON **83**

Name _____

More Congruency

Which one is not the same shape and same size as the others?

①

②

③

④

⑤

⑥

NOTE TO HOME
Students practice recognizing congruent
(same shape and same size) objects.

◆ **LESSON 83   More Congruency**

Solve these problems.

7 Jason had 75¢. If he spends 29¢, how much money will he have? _____ ¢

8 Leroy read 18 pages this morning. He read 27 pages this afternoon. How many pages did he read today? _____

9 Sumi has read 45 pages. Her book has 63 pages. How many more pages will she read to finish it? _____

Write your own word problems. Share them with a friend.

NOTE TO HOME
Students review solving two-digit addition and subtraction word problems.

Name _____

Patterns

Find a pattern. Fill in the blanks.

1 30, 27, 24, 21, 18, 15, _____, _____, _____, _____, 0

2 100, 95, 90, 85, _____, _____, _____, _____, _____, _____, 50

3 7, 14, 21, 28, _____, _____, _____, _____, _____, 70

4 70, 63, 56, 49, _____, _____, _____, _____, _____, _____, 0

5 1, 3, 5, 4, 6, 8, 7, 9, _____, _____, _____, _____, _____, 15

6 3, 6, 9, 7, 10, 13, 11, _____, _____, _____, _____, 21

7 2, 4, 6, 5, 7, 9, 8, 10, _____, _____, _____, _____, _____, 16

8 20, 17, 14, 16, 13, 10, 12, _____, _____, _____, _____, 2

NOTE TO HOME
Students identify and complete patterns.

◆ **LESSON 84** Patterns

Fill in the blanks.

9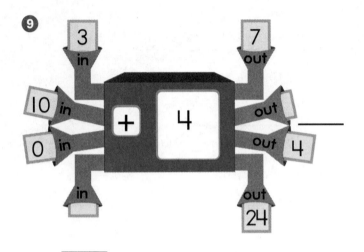

10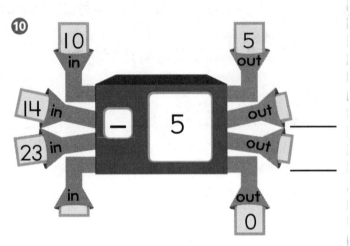

What is the rule? Write it in the box.

11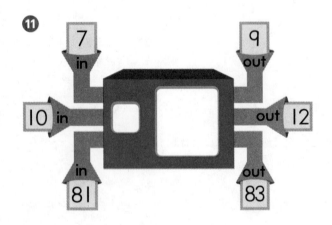

12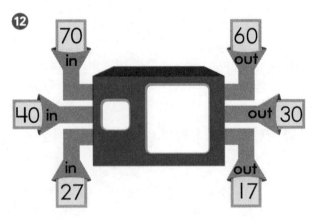

NOTE TO HOME
Students solve problems involving functions.

Function Tables

Name _____

Fill in the missing numbers.

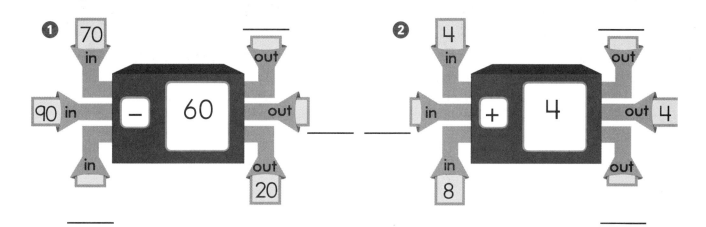

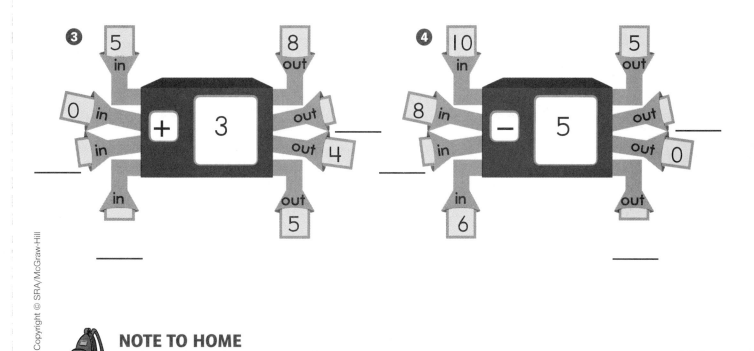

NOTE TO HOME
Students solve problems involving functions.

◆ **LESSON 85** **Function Tables**

Figure out the rule. Write it in the space.

5

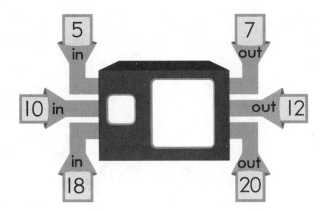

6

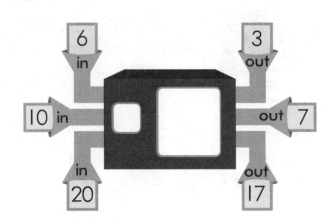

7

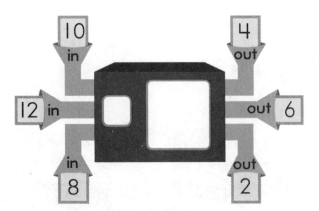

8

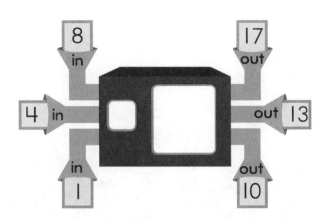

Play the "Function Rule" game.

NOTE TO HOME
Students figure out the function rules.

Name _____

Collecting Data

Object	How many
👫	ⅢⅡ ⅢⅡ ⅢⅡ ⅠⅠ
🚗	ⅢⅡ ⅢⅡ ⅢⅡ ⅢⅡ ⅢⅡ ⅠⅠⅠⅠ
🚚	ⅢⅡ ⅢⅡ ⅢⅡ Ⅰ
🚲	ⅢⅡ Ⅰ

1 How many people? _____

2 How many cars? _____

3 How many trucks? _____

4 How many bikes? _____

5 How many objects with wheels? _____

6 How many objects with motors? _____

7 How many all together? _____

Talk about the Thinking Story
"The Ten-Minute Wonder."

NOTE TO HOME
Students use tally marks to collect data.

Unit 2   Lesson 86 • **187**

◆ **LESSON 86 Collecting Data**

Work with friends. Collect data. Make up problems about your data.

Object	How many

NOTE TO HOME
Students collect and record data.

LESSON
87

Name _____

Measurement–
Thermometers

Count by twos. Fill in the blanks.

1. 50, 52, 54, _____, _____, 60

2. 0, 2, _____, _____, _____, 10

3. 70, _____, _____, _____, _____, 80

4. 20, _____, _____, _____, _____, 30

5. 100, 102, _____, _____, _____, 110

6. 30, _____, _____, _____, _____, 40

7. 90, _____, _____, _____, _____, 100

8. 10, _____, _____, _____, _____, 20

9. −10, −8, −6, _____, _____, 0

10. −40, −38, _____, _____, _____, −30

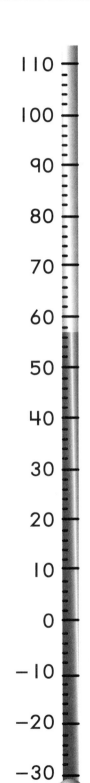

NOTE TO HOME
Students count by twos.

◆ **LESSON 87   Measurement—Thermometers**

Write the temperature.

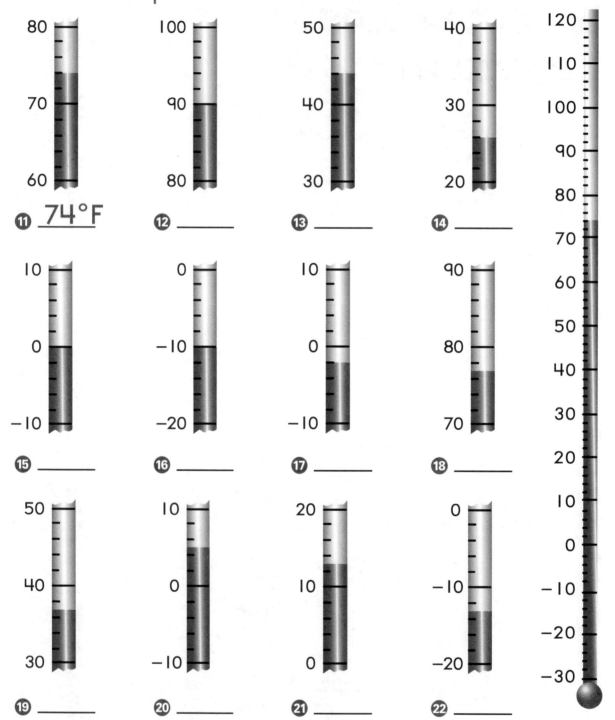

⑪ <u>74°F</u>   ⑫ _____   ⑬ _____   ⑭ _____

⑮ _____   ⑯ _____   ⑰ _____   ⑱ _____

⑲ _____   ⑳ _____   ㉑ _____   ㉒ _____

NOTE TO HOME
Students read a thermometer and count by twos.

LESSON 88

Name _____

Unit 2 Review

Lessons 50 to 55

Solve these problems. Watch the signs.

① 34
+27

② 34
−27

③ 83
−45

④ 29
+36

⑤ 64
+18

⑥ 33
+56

⑦ 56
−33

⑧ 75
−47

⑨ 12
− 8

⑩ 8
+12

⑪ 30
+27

⑫ 6
+78

Lessons 39 and 40

⑬ How long is the fish? _____ cm

NOTE TO HOME
Students review unit skills and concepts.

◆ **LESSON 88** **Unit 2 Review**

Lesson
70–72

What time is it?

⑭ _____ : _____

⑮ _____ : _____

Lesson
73–75

⑯ Color one third.

⑰ Color two fifths.

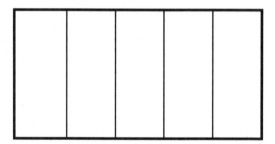

Lesson
56

⑱ Pablo has two dimes. An apple costs
12¢. How much change will Pablo get
if he buys an apple? _____ ¢

192 • Two-Digit Addition and Subtraction

NOTE TO HOME
Students review unit skills and concepts.

◆ **LESSON 88 Unit 2 Review**

Name _____

Lesson 56

⑲ Jack has 37¢. Jill has 54¢.

Who has more? _____

How much more? _____ ¢

How much do they have all together? _____¢

Slacks $18
Jacket $18
Hat $5

Lesson 63

⑳ Mrs. Davidson has $35.
Can she buy the jacket and slacks? _____

㉑ Suppose she buys the jacket.
How much money will she have left? $ _____

Lessons 19 and 20

Solve these problems.

㉒ ☐ + 3 = 10   ㉓ 6 + ☐ = 16

㉔ 5 + ☐ = 12   ㉕ 10 + ☐ = 17

㉖ 10 = ☐ + 1   ㉗ 12 = ☐ + 6

NOTE TO HOME
Students review unit skills and concepts.

◆ **LESSON 88** **Unit 2 Review**

Find the rule. Fill in the space.

Lessons 15 and 20

Rule	In	10	5	0		37
	Out	13	8		10	

Lesson 87

What is the temperature?

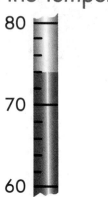

㉙ temperature _____ ° F ㉚ temperature _____ ° F

girls	𝍸𝍸 𝍸𝍸 III
boys	𝍸𝍸 𝍸𝍸 𝍸𝍸 I
women	𝍸𝍸 𝍸𝍸 II
men	𝍸𝍸 𝍸𝍸 IIII

Lesson 47

㉛ How many men? _____ ㉜ How many girls? _____

㉝ How many adults? _____ ㉞ How many children? _____

㉟ How many people? _____

NOTE TO HOME
Students review unit skills and concepts.

LESSON 89

Name _____

Unit 2 Test

Check your math skills.

How long? Use your ruler.

①  _____ cm

② _____ cm

Which are the same shape and same size as the first one?

③

④

What time is it?

⑤ _____ : _____   ⑥ _____ : _____

NOTE TO HOME
This test checks unit skills and concepts.

◆ **LESSON 89** Unit 2 Test

7 Color one fifth.

8 Color three fifths.

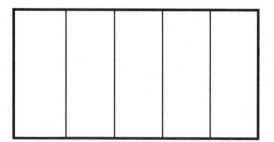

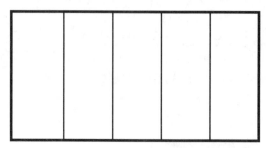

9 Color one quarter.

10 Color two thirds.

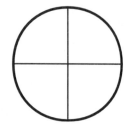

Solve these problems.

11 $4 + \boxed{} = 10$

12 $\boxed{} + 3 = 9$

13 $8 + \boxed{} = 16$

14 $\boxed{} + 9 = 19$

15 $75 - \boxed{} = 43$

16 $18 - \boxed{} = 3$

17 $26 - \boxed{} = 12$

18 $36 - \boxed{} = 29$

19 $47 - \boxed{} = 21$

20 $50 - \boxed{} = 50$

NOTE TO HOME
This test checks unit skills and concepts.

◆ **LESSON 89 Unit 2 Test**

Solve these problems.

㉑ Marie has 71¢. Paul has 49¢.

Who has more?

_____

How much more?
_____ ¢

㉒ How much for one bat and one ball?
$ _____

㉓ How much for two bats and one ball?
$ _____

㉔ How much for one glove and one ball?
$ _____

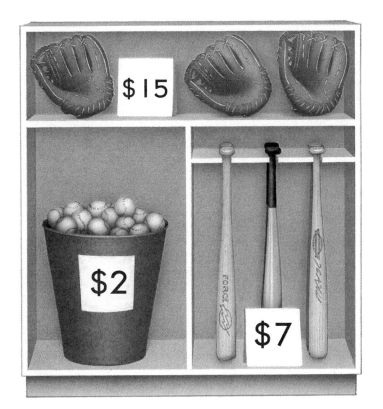

㉕ Fred planted 45 bean seeds. So far, 29 have sprouted.
How many have not sprouted? _____

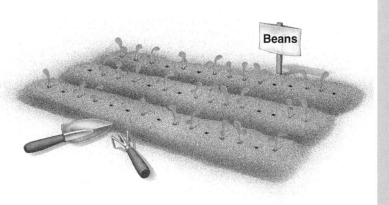

NOTE TO HOME
This test checks unit skills and concepts.

◆ **LESSON 89** **Unit 2 Test**

Watch the signs.

㉖   5
   + 7

㉗   8
   + 4

㉘   17
  − 9

㉙   16
  − 8

㉚   28
  +41

㉛   37
  −25

㉜   60
  −33

㉝   66
  −33

㉞   29
  +41

㉟   37
  −27

㊱   18
  +18

㊲   81
  −39

㊳   56
  −29

㊴   35
  +35

㊵   50
  −25

㊶   64
  +27

㊷   30
  +26

㊸   42
  +18

㊹   65
  −24

㊺   41
  −23

NOTE TO HOME
This test checks unit skills and concepts.

LESSON 90

Name _____

Extending the Unit

GAME

Play the "Roll a Problem" game.

Listen to the directions.

```
  ___ ___          ___ ___          ___ ___          ___ ___
+ ___ ___        + ___ ___        + ___ ___        + ___ ___
  ___ ___          ___ ___          ___ ___          ___ ___
```

```
  ___ ___          ___ ___          ___ ___          ___ ___
+ ___ ___        + ___ ___        + ___ ___        + ___ ___
  ___ ___          ___ ___          ___ ___          ___ ___
```

```
  ___ ___          ___ ___          ___ ___          ___ ___
- ___ ___        - ___ ___        - ___ ___        - ___ ___
  ___ ___          ___ ___          ___ ___          ___ ___
```

```
  ___ ___          ___ ___          ___ ___          ___ ___
- ___ ___        - ___ ___        - ___ ___        - ___ ___
  ___ ___          ___ ___          ___ ___          ___ ___
```

NOTE TO HOME
Students play a game to review skills in addition
and subtraction.

◆ **LESSON 90 Extending the Unit**

Solve the cross number puzzle.

1		▓	▓	2	
	▓	▓	3		▓
4	5	▓		▓	▓
▓	6	7	▓	8	9
▓	▓		▓	▓	

Across

❶ 9 + 8 = _____

❷ 90 − 49 = _____

❸ 9 + 7 = _____

❹ 16 − 16 = _____

❺ 52 − 44 = _____

❻ 83 − 18 = _____

❽ 89 − 36 = _____

Down

❶ 50 + 50 = _____

❷ 18 + 28 = _____

❸ 62 − 49 = _____

❺ 99 − 13 = _____

❼ 23 + 34 = _____

❾ 60 − 28 = _____

NOTE TO HOME
Students review addition and
subtraction skills.

200 • Two-Digit Addition and Subtraction

UNIT 3

Measurement

APPLYING AND ESTIMATING

- length, weight, and capacity

- approximation

- reading maps

- shapes

Carpenters use math . . .

The tools in this picture help carpenters measure and cut. Carpenters decide what shape pieces they need. Each piece is carefully measured and then cut from a larger piece of wood.

LESSON 91

Name _____

Less Than, Greater Than

What is the right sign? Draw <, >, or =.

1 10 ◯ 20

2 2 ◯ 1 + 1

3 5 ◯ 1 + 1

4 9 ◯ 4 + 3

5 56 ◯ 56

6 4 ◯ 5 + 5

7 12 ◯ 21

8 13 ◯ 10 + 3

9 87 ◯ 78

10 30 ◯ 14 + 3

11 55 ◯ 55

12 22 ◯ 20 + 2

13 0 ◯ 99

14 30 ◯ 20 + 20

15 41 ◯ 14

16 29 ◯ 25 + 4

17 81 ◯ 78

18 19 ◯ 91

NOTE TO HOME
Students use less than, greater than, and equal
signs to show how numbers are related.

Unit 3   Lesson 91 • **203**

◆ **LESSON 91** Less Than, Greater Than

What is the right sign? Draw <, >, or =.

19. $9 + 8 \bigcirc 7 + 9$ 20. $41 + 3 \bigcirc 49$

21. $2 + 3 \bigcirc 2 + 4$ 22. $21 - 4 \bigcirc 17$

23. $20 + 3 \bigcirc 20 + 4$ 24. $6 + 15 \bigcirc 19$

25. $5 - 3 \bigcirc 5 - 4$ 26. $58 - 7 \bigcirc 49$

27. $28 - 3 \bigcirc 28 - 4$ 28. $24 + 5 \bigcirc 28$

29. $5 + 6 \bigcirc 6 + 5$ 30. $15 + 16 \bigcirc 32$

31. $10 + 3 \bigcirc 10 + 4$ 32. $61 - 3 \bigcirc 57$

33. $87 + 3 \bigcirc 87 + 4$ 34. $18 + 9 \bigcirc 25$

35. $10 - 3 \bigcirc 10 - 4$ 36. $37 - 7 \bigcirc 30$

THINKING STORY

Talk about the Thinking Story "Ferdie Borrows and Borrows and Borrows."

NOTE TO HOME
Students show number relationships with less than, greater than, or equal signs.

204 • Measurement

LESSON
92

Name _____

Three Addends

Add.

❶   5
     8
  + 4
  ____

❷   7
     3
  + 8
  ____

❸   4
     8
  + 6
  ____

❹   5
     6
  + 7
  ____

❺   8
     9
  +4
  ____

❻   14
     10
  + 26
  ____

❼   13
     12
  + 14
  ____

❽   21
     34
  + 13
  ____

❾   21
     18
  + 16
  ____

❿   36
     23
  +12
  ____

GAME

Play the "Roll a Problem" game.

___ ___
___ ___
+ ___ ___
_____

___ ___
___ ___
+ ___ ___
_____

⓫   19
     24
  + 20
  ____

___ ___
___ ___
+ ___ ___
_____

___ ___
___ ___
+ ___ ___
_____

⓬   31
     18
  + 27
  ____

NOTE TO HOME
Students learn to add three two-digit numbers.

Unit 3   Lesson 92 • **205**

◆ **LESSON 92   Three Addends**

Add. Use shortcuts if you can.

⑬   27
     26
  + 39

⑭   18
     24
  + 15

⑮   25
     25
  + 25

⑯   24
     25
  + 26

⑰   13
     20
  +67

⑱   23
     25
  + 27

⑲   20
     25
  + 30

⑳   30
     16
  + 28

㉑   42
     13
  + 17

㉒   18
     53
  +10

March has 31 days.
April has 30 days.
May has 31 days.

㉓ How many days are in March,
  April, and May all together? _____

NOTE TO HOME
Students continue adding three
two-digit numbers.

LESSON
93

Name _____

Telling Time—
Nearest Half Hour

What time is it?

① __7__ : __00__

② ____ : ____

③ ____ : ____

④ ____ : ____

⑤ ____ : ____

⑥ ____ : ____

⑦ ____ : ____

⑧ ____ : ____

⑨ ____ : ____

NOTE TO HOME
Students practice telling time to the half hour.

◆ **LESSON 93** Telling Time—Nearest Half Hour

About what time is it? The hands might
not be at exactly that time.

Tell the time to the nearest half hour.

⑩ __2__ : __00__ ⑪ _____ : _____ ⑫ _____ : _____

⑬ _____ : _____ ⑭ _____ : _____ ⑮ _____ : _____

⑯ _____ : _____ ⑰ _____ : _____ ⑱ _____ : _____

One day on Mercury lasts as long as
about eight Earth years.

NOTE TO HOME
Students tell time to the nearest half hour.

LESSON 94

Name _____

Telling Time— To the Minute

What time is it?

1 _____ : _____

2 _____ : _____

3 _____ : _____

4 _____ : _____

5 _____ : _____

6 _____ : _____

7 _____ : _____

8 _____ : _____

NOTE TO HOME
Students learn to tell time to the nearest minute.

Unit 3   Lesson 94 • **209**

◆ LESSON 94 Telling Time—To the Minute

Draw the minute hands.

9 3:27

10 4:51

11 8:04

12 10:40

Copyright © SRA/McGraw-Hill

NOTE TO HOME
Students continue to tell time
to the nearest minute.

Name _____

Telling Time— Before the Hour

What time is it?

1 _____ : _____

2 _____ : _____

3 _____ : _____

4 _____ : _____

5 _____ : _____

6 _____ : _____

7 _____ : _____

8 _____ : _____

NOTE TO HOME
Students practice telling time to the nearest minute.

Unit 3   Lesson 95 • **211**

◆ **LESSON 95** Telling Time—Before the Hour

How many minutes before the hour?

9 __15__ minutes before __1__   **10** _____ minutes before _____

11 _____ minutes before _____   **12** _____ minutes before _____

13 _____ minutes before _____   **14** _____ minutes before _____

15 _____ minutes before _____   **16** _____ minutes before _____

NOTE TO HOME
Students learn to tell how many minutes
before the hour a clock shows.

LESSON
96

Name _____

Keeping Sharp

Solve these problems. Watch the signs.

① 5
    + 6

② 4
    + 9

③ 8
    + 7

④ 9
    + 9

⑤ 15
    − 8

⑥ 13
    − 9

⑦ 12
    − 3

⑧ 9
    − 2

Solve.

⑨ 83
    + 72

⑩ 26
    + 38

⑪ 47
    + 83

⑫ 32
    + 69

⑬ 98
    − 35

⑭ 153
    − 28

⑮ 64
    − 37

⑯ 56
    − 27

NOTE TO HOME
Students review skills presented in this unit.

◆ **LESSON 96   Keeping Sharp**

Solve these problems.

⑰ ☐ = 4 + 4   ⑱ ☐ + 5 = 14

⑲ ☐ + 8 = 17   ⑳ 10 = ☐ + 6

㉑ 10 + ☐ = 13   ㉒ 14 = 7 + ☐

What is the right sign? Draw <, >, or =.

㉓   8 + 9 ◯ 15   ㉔ 25 + 35 ◯ 100

㉕   45 − 25 ◯ 30   ㉖ 50 + 50 ◯ 100

㉗ 1000 − 100 ◯ 800   ㉘ 10 + 7 ◯ 17

㉙ 400 + 300 ◯ 700   ㉚ 100 − 50 ◯ 75

NOTE TO HOME
Students review skills presented in this unit.

◆ **LESSON 96 Keeping Sharp**

Name _____

Solve each problem two ways.

31 Color $\frac{3}{4}$.

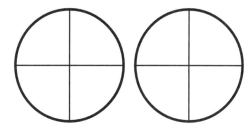

32 Color $\frac{1}{2}$.

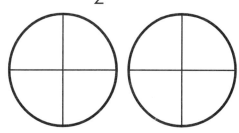

33 Color $\frac{2}{5}$.

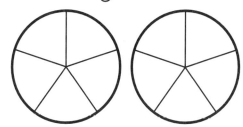

34 Color $\frac{1}{3}$.

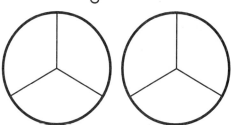

Work these problems. Watch the signs.

35	**36**	**37**	**38**	**39**
66	43	81	30	21
+ 23	+ 59	− 22	− 29	+ 18

40	**41**	**42**	**43**	**44**
24	46	27	19	31
19	21	16	9	18
+ 20	+ 18	+ 17	+ 15	+ 27

NOTE TO HOME
Students review skills presented in this unit.

◆ **LESSON 96   Keeping Sharp**

Add.

⑤ $7 + 8 + 9 =$ _____

㊻ $12 + 15 + 7 =$ _____

㊼ $21 + 10 + 15 =$ _____

㊽ $5 + 35 + 18 =$ _____

㊾ $11 + 32 + 25 =$ _____

㊿ $17 + 17 + 6 =$ _____

51 $4 + 9 + 6 =$ _____

52 $23 + 19 + 22 =$ _____

What time is it?

53 _____ : _____

54 _____ : _____

55 _____ : _____

56 _____ : _____

57 _____ : _____

58 _____ : _____

NOTE TO HOME
Students review skills presented in this unit.

LESSON 97

Name _____

Column Addition

Solve these problems. Use shortcuts if you can.

①
```
  42
  86
+ 74
```

②
```
  98
  76
+ 85
```

③
```
  34
  29
+ 16
```

④
```
  33
  53
+ 34
```

⑤
```
  33
  33
  34
+ 34
```

⑥
```
  25
  25
  25
+ 25
```

⑦
```
  17
  32
  21
+ 13
```

⑧
```
  34
  63
  20
+ 12
```

⑨
```
  76
  89
  12
+ 96
```

⑩
```
  54
  87
  69
+ 94
```

⑪
```
  75
  75
  75
+ 75
```

⑫
```
  30
  30
  26
+ 17
```

THINKING STORY

Talk about the Thinking Story "I Owe You."

NOTE TO HOME
Students review adding columns
of two-digit numbers.

◆ **LESSON 97   Column Addition**

Solve these problems.

13 Mary worked four weeks during the summer.
The chart shows how much money she earned.
How much money did Mary earn? $_____

Week	Amount Earned
1	$87
2	$65
3	$58
4	$73

14 How far is it from *A* to *B* to *C* to *D* to *E*
and back to *A*? _____

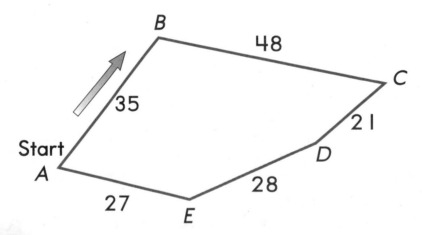

Play the "Roll a Problem" game.

NOTE TO HOME
Students continue reviewing two-digit
addition.

LESSON
98

Name _____

Column Addition—
Finding Perimeter

Solve these problems.

1 This is part of Mr. Mason's yard. He wants to put a fence around it. What is the perimeter of the yard?

_____ meters

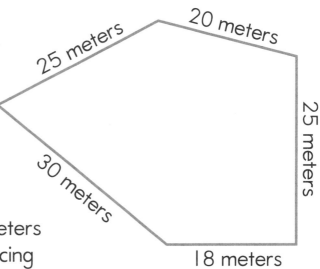

25 meters

20 meters

25 meters

30 meters

18 meters

2 Each roll of fencing is 25 meters long. How many rolls of fencing does Mr. Mason need?

_____

3 The town of Muddleville began 96 years ago. There are 87 people now living in Muddleville. There are also 42 cats in Muddleville.

How many dogs are there in Muddleville? _____

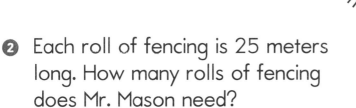

NOTE TO HOME
Students practice solving word problems.

◆ **LESSON 98** Column Addition—Finding Perimeter

Add.

④   64
      27
      59
  + 12

⑤   17
      46
      73
  + 59

⑥   40
      40
      40
  + 40

⑦   10
      20
      30
  + 40

⑧   34
      20
  + 20

⑨   58
      30
  + 10

⑩   66
      20
      20
  + 10

⑪   22
      33
      11
  + 10

⑫   23
      50
      10
  + 28

⑬   29
      79
      88
  + 46

⑭   10
      97
      30
  + 56

⑮   18
      16
      40
  + 17

NOTE TO HOME
Students continue practicing
two-digit column addition.

Name _____

Mid-Unit Review

What is the right sign? Draw <, >, or =.

① 30 ◯ 40

② 7 ◯ 3 + 4

③ 65 ◯ 56

④ 8 ◯ 3 + 3

Add.

⑤
```
   6
   3
+  4
____
```

⑥
```
   8
   4
+  2
____
```

⑦
```
  22
  37
+ 16
____
```

⑧
```
  45
  16
+ 29
____
```

About what time is it? The hands might not be at exactly that time.

Tell the time to the nearest half hour.

⑨ _____ : _____

⑩ _____ : _____

⑪ _____ : _____

NOTE TO HOME
Students review unit skills and concepts.

◆ **UNIT 3 Mid-Unit Review**

What time is it?

12 _____ : _____

13 _____ : _____

14 Draw in the minute hands to show 5:42.

How many minutes before the hour?

15 _____ minutes before _____

16 _____ minutes before _____

Add.

17	**18**	**19**	**20**
73	35	50	41
48	26	30	18
39	42	5	29
+ 22	+ 31	+ 40	+ 4

🎒 **NOTE TO HOME**
Students review unit skills and concepts.

LESSON
99

Name _____

Reading Maps

GEOGRAPHY
CONNECTION

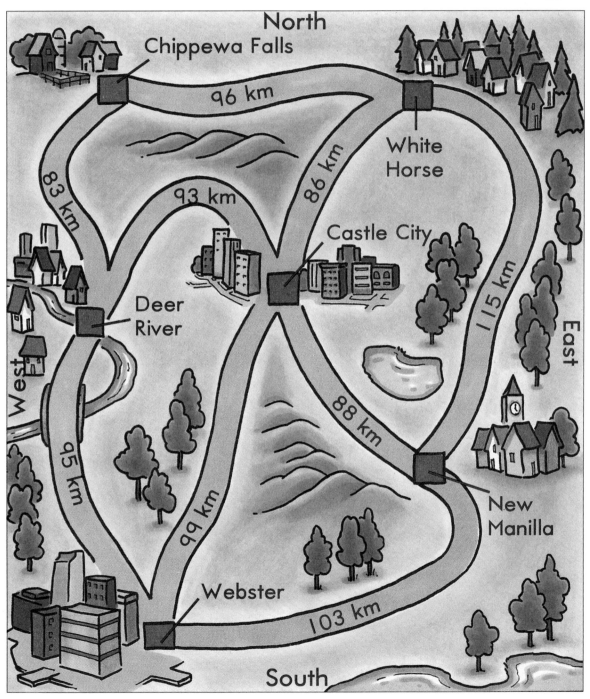

NOTE TO HOME
Students learn to read maps.

◆ **LESSON 99 Reading Maps**

GEOGRAPHY CONNECTION

Complete the chart. Use the map on page 223 to find the shortest distances.

	Towns	Shortest Distance (kilometers)
❶	Chippewa Falls and New Manilla	
❷	New Manilla and Deer River	
❸	White Horse and Webster	
❹	Chippewa Falls and Webster	

❺ What town is farthest from Castle City? _____

❻ What town is farthest from Webster? _____

❼ What town is closest to White Horse? _____

❽ What town is closest to Deer River? _____

❾ What is the shortest way to get to
Deer River from White Horse? _____

_____

GAME

Play the "Map" game.

NOTE TO HOME
Students learn to read maps.

LESSON
100

Name _____

Map Reading

GEOGRAPHY CONNECTION

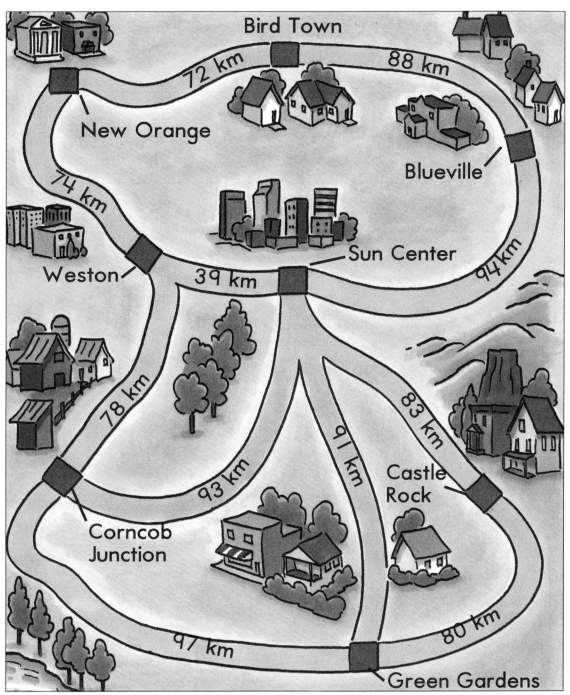

NOTE TO HOME
Students practice reading maps.

◆ LESSON 100 Map Reading

Complete the chart. Use the map on page 225 to find the shortest distances.

	Towns	Shortest Distance (kilometers)
❶	Blueville and New Orange	
❷	Bird Town and Corncob Junction	
❸	Castle Rock and Corncob Junction	
❹	Green Gardens and New Orange	

❺ Which town is closest to Corncob Junction? _____

❻ Which town is closest to Weston? _____

❼ Which town is closest to Sun Center? _____

❽ Which town is farthest from Weston? _____

❾ Which town will you pass through on
the road from New Orange to Blueville? _____

❿ Take a drive from Corncob Junction
through Green Gardens, Sun Center,
Weston, and back to Corncob Junction.

How far did you drive? _____ km

NOTE TO HOME
Students solve word problems that
involve reading maps.

LESSON
101

Name _____

Exploring Triangles

Measure the sides of each triangle in centimeters.
Add the lengths of the two shorter sides.
Then write the problem.

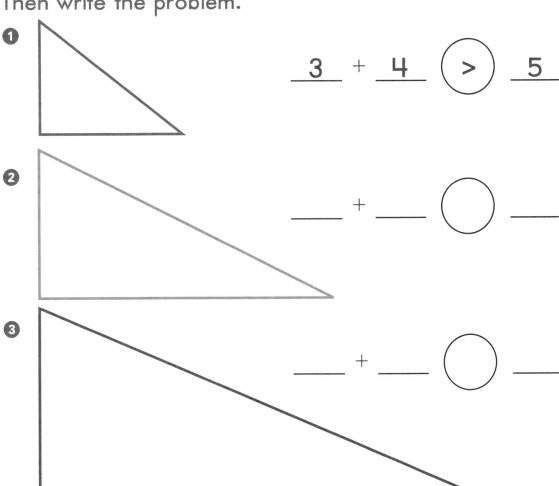

1 ___3___ + ___4___ (**>**) ___5___

2 ___ + ___ ( ) ___

3 ___ + ___ ( ) ___

4 Try to make a triangle with strips of paper 9 cm,
6 cm, and 5 cm long.

5 Now try to make another triangle with strips
9 cm, 4 cm, and 3 cm long.

NOTE TO HOME
Students explore properties of the sides
of triangles.

Unit 3   Lesson 101 • **227**

◆ **LESSON 101   Exploring Triangles**

What is the right sign? Draw <, >, or =.
Is it possible to make a triangle?

6 3 + 4 (>) 5   (yes)   no

7 4 + 6 ( ) 5   yes   no

8 2 + 10 ( ) 10   yes   no

9 1 + 10 ( ) 10   yes   no

10 5 + 6 ( ) 10   yes   no

11 5 + 5 ( ) 10   yes   no

12 3 + 4 ( ) 10   yes   no

13 6 + 6 ( ) 6   yes   no

NOTE TO HOME
Students continue to explore properties
of triangles.

228 • Measurement

LESSON 102

Name _____

Odd and Even Numbers

Ring the odd numbers.
Then write half of each even number.

1. 10 _____   2. 11 _____   3. 12 _____   4. 13 _____

5. 14 _____   6. 15 _____   7. 16 _____   8. 17 _____

9. 18 _____   10. 19 _____   11. 20 _____   12. 21 _____

13. 0 _____   14. 1 _____   15. 4 _____   16. 5 _____

17. 8 _____   18. 9 _____   19. 31 _____   20. 32 _____

21. 41 _____   22. 42 _____   23. 2 _____   24. 3 _____

25. 6 _____   26. 7 _____   27. 25 _____   28. 26 _____

29. 28 _____   30. 29 _____   31. 35 _____   32. 36 _____

A golf ball has more than 400 "dimples."

NOTE TO HOME
Students explore properties of odd and even numbers.

Unit 3   Lesson 102 • **229**

◆ **LESSON 102 Odd and Even Numbers**

Odds-Evens

Players: Two
Materials: Ten counters

RULES

First Player: You are the "even" player. Choose a number between 0 and 5. Put one hand behind your back with that many fingers extended.

Second Player: You are the "odd" player. Choose a number between 0 and 5. Put one hand behind your back with that many fingers extended.

Both Players: Count "1, 2, 3." Both of you bring your fingers to the front.

Winner: If the total number of fingers showing is even, the "even" player wins. If the total number of fingers showing is odd, the "odd" wins.

NOTE TO HOME
Students identify odd and even numbers through ten.

LESSON
103

Name _____

Odds and Evens

Ring the odd numbers.

1. 3   8   7   12   28

2. 41   50   56   59   63

Add. Then ring all the odd numbers.

3. $6 + ⑤ = \underline{(11)}$ 4. $2 + 2 = \underline{\qquad}$

5. $3 + 3 = \underline{\qquad}$ 6. $7 + 8 = \underline{\qquad}$

7. $9 + 7 = \underline{\qquad}$ 8. $5 + 7 = \underline{\qquad}$

9. $10 + 5 = \underline{\qquad}$ 10. $6 + 6 = \underline{\qquad}$

11. $20 + 7 = \underline{\qquad}$ 12. $7 + 7 = \underline{\qquad}$

13. $29 + 10 = \underline{\qquad}$ 14. $8 + 8 = \underline{\qquad}$

15. $17 + 14 = \underline{\qquad}$ 16. $12 + 12 = \underline{\qquad}$

17. $6 + 9 = \underline{\qquad}$ 18. $5 + 5 = \underline{\qquad}$

NOTE TO HOME
Students explore properties of odd and
even numbers.

Unit 3   Lesson 103 • **231**

◆ **LESSON 103 Odds and Evens**

19 Ring the even numbers.

| 0 | 1 | 2 | 3 | 4 | 5 | 6 | 7 | 8 | 9 |

| 10 | 11 | 12 | 13 | 14 | 15 | 16 | 17 | 18 | 19 |

| 20 | 21 | 22 | 23 | 24 | 25 | 26 | 27 | 28 | 29 |

Do you see a pattern? Can you use this pattern to decide whether a number is even?

20 Ring the even numbers.

60   88   97   100   247   356   482   611   998

21 Ring the odd numbers.

3   7   12   28   41   50   56   59   63

Add. Then ring all the odd numbers.

22 $6 + 5 = $ _____

23 $5 + 7 = $ _____

24 $2 + 2 = $ _____

25 $10 + 5 = $ _____

26 $3 + 3 = $ _____

27 $7 + 7 = $ _____

28 $7 + 8 = $ _____

29 $29 + 10 = $ _____

30 $9 + 7 = $ _____

31 $8 + 8 = $ _____

NOTE TO HOME
Students explore properties of odd and even numbers.

Name _____

Adding Odds and Evens

Think: even + even = even
odd + odd = even
even + odd = odd
odd + even = odd

Ring each wrong answer.
(Eight of the answers are wrong.)

❶ 18 + 26 = **44**   ❷ 41 + 23 = **75**

❸ 37 + 58 = **94**   ❹ 67 + 22 = **89**

❺ 39 + 39 = **78**   ❻ 54 + 19 = **73**

❼ 47 + 35 = **83**   ❽ 35 + 47 = **83**

❾ 45 + 45 = **90**   ❿ 78 + 19 = **96**

⓫ 17 + 58 = **74**   ⓬ 35 + 28 = **62**

⓭ 35 + 35 = **70**   ⓮ 8 + 77 = **86**

NOTE TO HOME
Students continue to explore properties
of odd and even numbers.

◆ **LESSON 104   Adding Odds and Evens**

Ring the odd numbers.

⑮   3   6   9   12   15   18   21

⑯   7   10   13   16   19   22   25

⑰   2   5   8   11   14   17   20

Solve the problems. Ring the odd number answers.

⑱ Rico has 24 crayons.
   If he loses 15 of them,
   how many will be left?

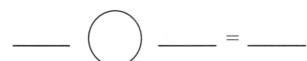

_____ ◯ _____ = _____

⑲ Ashley has 32 jumbo crayons and 48 small
   crayons. How many crayons in all?

_____ ◯ _____ = _____

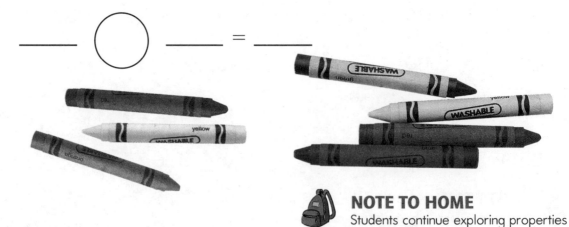

NOTE TO HOME
Students continue exploring properties
of odd and even numbers.

Name _____

Subtracting Odds and Evens

Use what you know about odd and even numbers. Ring each wrong answer. (Ten of the answers are wrong.)

1 $43 - 29 = 15$

2 $86 - 34 = 53$

3 $27 - 6 = 21$

4 $82 - 13 = 58$

5 $93 - 6 = 77$

6 $100 - 35 = 66$

7 $100 - 27 = 73$

8 $81 - 59 = 22$

9 $50 - 18 = 33$

10 $84 - 25 = 58$

11 $65 - 37 = 29$

12 $100 - 25 = 75$

13 $83 - 30 = 53$

14 $60 - 54 = 6$

15 $27 - 24 = 50$

16 $39 - 19 = 21$

NOTE TO HOME
Students continue to explore properties of even and odd numbers.

◆ **LESSON 105** **Subtracting Odds and Evens**

Ring each wrong answer.
(Five of the answers are wrong.)

⑰ 48 + 69 106	⑱ 73 + 81 154	⑲ 94 − 27 67	⑳ 83 + 72 155
㉑ 96 − 81 15	㉒ 42 + 98 140	㉓ 50 + 50 100	㉔ 26 + 38 64
㉕ 87 − 69 18	㉖ 73 + 86 158	㉗ 90 − 78 21	㉘ 98 − 35 63
㉙ 90 − 76 14	㉚ 75 + 25 95	㉛ 43 − 41 2	㉜ 47 + 83 131

THINKING STORY

Talk about the Thinking Story "Sharing with Cousin Trixie."

NOTE TO HOME
Students continue to use what they know about odd and even numbers.

LESSON
106

Name _____

Kilograms and Grams

The kilogram and the gram are units of weight.
There are 1000 grams in 1 kilogram.

How many?

1 1 kilogram = _____ grams

2 2 kg = _____ g

3 3 kg = _____ g

4 4 kg = _____ g

5 10 kg = _____ g

6 5 kg = _____ g

NOTE TO HOME
Students learn how grams and
kilograms are related.

◆ **LESSON 106 Kilograms and Grams**

COOPERATIVE LEARNING

How much does it weigh?

Unit _____

Objects	Estimate Weight	Measure Weight	Difference

One ton of recycled waste paper saves 17 trees.

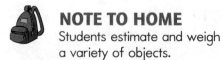

NOTE TO HOME
Students estimate and weigh
a variety of objects.

238 • Measurement

LESSON
107

Name _____

Pounds and Ounces

The pound and the ounce are units of weight.
There are 16 ounces in 1 pound.

Ring the better answers.

1 How many ounces in a pound?   1 ounces   16 ounces

2 How much does one grape weigh?   1 pound   1 ounce

3 How much does a book weigh?   1 pound   1 ounce

4 How much does a pencil weigh?   more than 1 pound

less than 1 pound

5 How much do you weigh?   more than 1 pound

less than 1 pound

NOTE TO HOME
Students estimate using pounds and ounces.

Unit 3   Lesson 107 • **239**

◆ **LESSON 107 Pounds and Ounces**

feathers   bricks   clothes

6 Which box weighs the most? _____

7 Which box weighs the least? _____

Becky weighs more than Libby but less than Goldie.

8 Who weighs the most? _____

9 Who weighs the least? _____

Martin weighs 112 pounds. Mollie weighs 118 pounds. Maris weighs 99 pounds.

10 Who weighs the most? _____

11 Who weighs the least? _____

NOTE TO HOME
Students compare weights.

LESSON
108

Name _____

Using Measurements

Solve these problems.

1 The branch is 100 inches from the ground. The swing is 30 inches from the ground. About how many inches of rope were used to tie the swing to the branch? _____

2 Caroline needs 60 meters of rope. Rope comes in packages of 25 meters. How many packages must she buy? _____

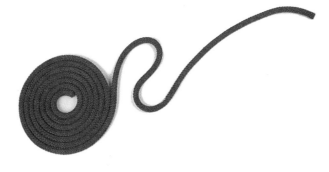

Do the "Making a Kilogram" activity.

NOTE TO HOME
Students solve problems about measurement.

◆ **LESSON 108   Using Measurements**

Compare methods of solving. Which do you think is easiest?

What is the right sign? Draw <, >, or =.

3   10 〇 15   **4**   17 − 7 〇 18 − 18

5   16 + 1 〇 16 + 2   **6**   122 + 23 〇 122 + 20

7   18 − 1 〇 18 − 5   **8**   195 − 95 〇 195 − 96

9   25 + 25 〇 25 + 26   **10**   75 + 75 〇 75 + 75

11   25 〇 52   **12**   18 + 2 〇 2 + 18

13   89 + 5 〇 89 + 10   **14**   19 + 3 〇 0 + 19

15   6 + 125 〇 125 + 6   **16**   35 − 1 〇 35 − 5

17   999 〇 998 + 1   **18**   675 + 1 〇 675 + 0

NOTE TO HOME
Students review using less than,
greater than, and equal signs.

LESSON **109**

Name _____

Measurement—Capacity

16 fluid ounces = 1 pint

2 pints = 1 quart

4 quarts = 1 gallon

How many?

1 How many fluid ounces in 1 quart? _____

2 How many pints in 1 gallon? _____

3 How many fluid ounces in 1 gallon? _____

4 How many fluid ounces in 2 gallons? _____

5 How many fluid ounces in 3 gallons? _____

6 How many fluid ounces in 4 quarts? _____

7 How many pints in 4 quarts? _____

NOTE TO HOME
Students convert customary units of volume (capacity).

Unit 3   Lesson 109 • **243**

◆ **LESSON 109** Measurement—Capacity

A pint of water weighs about 1 pound.

How much?

8 How much does a quart of water weigh? _____ pounds

9 How much does a gallon of water weigh? _____ pounds

10 How much do 5 gallons of water weigh? _____ pounds

11 How many ounces in a pound? _____

12 How many fluid ounces in a pint? _____

13 How much do you think a
fluid ounce of water weighs? _____

GAME

Play the "Measurement" game.

NOTE TO HOME
Students convert customary units
of volume (capacity).

Name _____

Metric Measurement— Capacity

1000 milliliters = 1 liter

1 cubic centimeter = 1 milliliter

1 cubic decimeter = 1 liter

Use a centimeter ruler.

❶ Draw a square centimeter.

❷ Draw a square decimeter (10 cm on a side).

NOTE TO HOME
Students review metric capacity.

◆ **LESSON 110 Metric Measurement—Capacity**

A liter is a little more than a quart.

How many?

❸ About how many pints are in a liter? _____

❹ About how many liters are in a gallon? _____

A liter of water weighs 1 kilogram.

How much?

❺ How much does a
milliliter of water weigh? _____

❻ How much do
5 liters of water weigh? _____

❼ Sara is having a party. She
needs about two gallons of punch.
The punch she wants is in liter bottles.
How many liters of punch should she buy? _____

246 • Measurement

NOTE TO HOME
Students review metric capacity.

LESSON
111

Name _____

Using Measurements

① How many can safely ride in this boat at one time? _____

② How many can safely ride in this boat at one time? _____

③ Green Pond is 80 meters long. Ginny
knows she can swim 250 meters. Can
she swim to the end of the pond and back? _____

THINKING STORY

Talk about the Thinking Story "More
Sharing with Cousin Trixie."

NOTE TO HOME
Students solve problems involving measurement.

◆ **LESSON 111 Using Measurement**

Solve these problems.

④ You need 25 gallons of paint. Each can holds
10 gallons. How many cans must you buy?

_____

⑤ You need 12 cups of juice. Each box holds 8 cups.
How many boxes of juice must you buy?

_____

⑥ Spencer's dog Rover is 65 centimeters
tall. The bottom of the window is
92 centimeters from the floor. The stool
is 30 centimeters high. Can Rover look out
the window if he stands on the stool?

_____

⑦ A pitcher can hold one gallon. How many
quarts of juice will the pitcher hold?

_____

⑧ At football practice Bryan must run 50 yards.
He has run 32 yards. How many more
yards must he run?

_____

NOTE TO HOME
Students solve problems about measuring
capacity and length.

LESSON
112

Name _____

Shortcuts

Add.

$$37 + 19$$

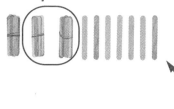

1 Is 37 + 19 the same as 36 + 20? _____

2 37 + 19 = _____

$$37 - 19$$

Subtract 20; put 1 back.

3 Is 37 − 19 the same as 38 − 20? _____

4 37 − 19 = _____

Use shortcuts to solve these problems.

5 56 + 29 = _____   **6** 63 + 19 = _____

7 54 + 39 = _____   **8** 56 − 29 = _____

9 63 − 19 = _____   **10** 54 − 39 = _____

NOTE TO HOME
Students learn shortcuts to two-digit
addition and subtraction.

◆ **LESSON 112 Shortcuts**

Solve these problems. Use shortcuts when
you can.

⑪ 91 − 89 = _____   ⑫ 38 + 42 = _____

⑬ 91 − 39 = _____   ⑭ 38 + 47 = _____

⑮ 92 − 89 = _____   ⑯ 28 + 32 = _____

⑰ 92 − 39 = _____   ⑱ 28 + 37 = _____

⑲ 73 + 19 = _____   ⑳ 81 − 39 = _____

㉑ 23 + 19 = _____   ㉒ 51 − 38 = _____

㉓ 46 + 39 = _____   ㉔ 51 − 39 = _____

㉕ 46 + 38 = _____   ㉖ 52 − 38 = _____

㉗ 46 + 37 = _____   ㉘ 47 − 27 = _____

Talk about the ways you did these.

Describe your shortcuts. What works best
for you?

NOTE TO HOME
Students use shortcuts to two-digit
addition and subtraction.

LESSON 113

Name _____

Round to Ten

Round to the nearest ten.

1. 73 _____   2. 84 _____   3. 99 _____

4. 7 _____   5. 3 _____   6. 6 _____

7. 54 _____   8. 90 _____   9. 56 _____

10. 61 _____   11. 88 _____   12. 12 _____

13. 35 _____   14. 55 _____   15. 15 _____

16. 73 _____   17. 42 _____   18. 5 _____

19. 8 _____   20. 39 _____   21. 17 _____

22. 66 _____   23. 22 _____   24. 48 _____

Is 35 closer to 30 or to 40?
Talk about it.

NOTE TO HOME
Students round to tens.

◆ **LESSON 113   Round to Ten**

Estimate answers to the nearest ten. Then
calculate the difference between your
estimate and the exact answer.

	Estimate	Exact answer	Difference
25 42 + 38 = _____		_____	_____
26 72 − 28 = _____		_____	_____
27 81 − 19 = _____		_____	_____
28 71 + 19 = _____		_____	_____
29 45 − 25 = _____		_____	_____
30 45 + 25 = _____		_____	_____
31 33 + 43 = _____		_____	_____
32 87 − 56 = _____		_____	_____
33 48 + 69 = _____		_____	_____
34 87 − 63 = _____		_____	_____

NOTE TO HOME
Students estimate answers by rounding to ten.

LESSON 114

Name _____

Unit 3 Review

What time is it?

Lessons 93–95

1 _____:_____   **2** _____:_____   **3** _____:_____

Lessons 73–75

4 Color three fourths.

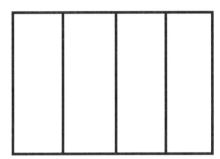

5 Color one third.

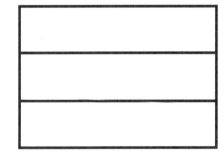

What is the right sign? Draw <, >, or =.

Lesson 91

6 8 + 7 ◯ 20   **7** 112 ◯ 84 + 112

8 14 + 26 ◯ 26 + 14   **9** 127 ◯ 100 + 27

NOTE TO HOME
Students review unit skills and concepts.

◆ **LESSON 114   Unit 3 Review**

Lessons
102–105

10 Ring the odd numbers.

3   22   10   195   86

47   73   351   98   352

Solve these problems.

Lessons
104 and
105

11 ☐ = 10 + 4   **12** ☐ = 10 − 4

13 5 + ☐ = 13   **14** ☐ + 8 = 17

15 12 = ☐ + 7   **16** 14 = 5 + ☐

Lesson
112

Solve the problems. Watch the signs.

17 20   **18** 26   **19** 91   **20** 53
     − 19   + 18   − 84   + 29

The longest hiccup attack lasted five years.

NOTE TO HOME
Students review unit skills and concepts.

◆ **LESSON 114   Unit 3 Review**   Name _____

Solve these problems.

Lessons   ㉑ George is 53 inches tall. Paula is 48
67 and   inches tall.
68
                   Who is taller? _____

                   How much taller? _____ inches

㉒ Mrs. Okomoto works in sales.
   She drove 75 miles on
   Monday, 30 miles
   on Tuesday, and
   63 miles on
   Wednesday. How far
   did she drive in the three days?

   _____ miles

㉓ Mr. Katz has $49. He wants
   to buy a sweater that costs
   $85. How much more does
   he need?

   $ _____

㉔ There are 100 centimeters in 1 meter.
   How many centimeters are there in 7 meters? _____

NOTE TO HOME
Students review unit skills and concepts.

◆ **LESSON 114 Unit 3 Review**

Solve these problems. Use shortcuts
when you can.

Lesson
96

25 13 + 17 = _____

26 76 − 59 = _____

27 18 + 17 = _____

28 58 − 28 = _____

29 59 + 38 = _____

30 35 − 26 = _____

31 39 + 43 = _____

32 64 − 49 = _____

33 38 + 43 = _____

34 64 − 19 = _____

Estimate answers by rounding to the nearest
ten. Then calculate the difference between
your estimate and the exact answer.

	Estimate	Exact answer	Difference
Lesson 113			
35 66 − 39 =	_____	_____	_____
36 18 + 53 =	_____	_____	_____
37 45 + 55 =	_____	_____	_____
38 71 − 64 =	_____	_____	_____

NOTE TO HOME
Students continue to review skills
presented in this unit.

LESSON
115

Name _____

Unit 3 Test

Check your math skills.

Solve these problems. Watch the signs.

1   8 + 9 = _____   **2**   15 − 7 = _____

3   16 − 6 = _____   **4**   8 + 2 = _____

5   12 − 3 = _____   **6**   5 + 7 = _____

7   8 + ☐ = 12   **8**   ☐ + 7 = 11

9   18 = 9 + ☐   **10**   12 = ☐ + 6

11   ☐ + 0 = 7   **12**   9 + ☐ = 9

13   ☐ = 5 + 5   **14**   ☐ + 3 = 13

15   Ring the odd numbers.

    1   8   123   500   501

NOTE TO HOME
This test checks unit skills and concepts.

◆ **LESSON 115** Unit 3 Test

Solve these problems. Watch the signs.

⑯   24   ⑰   36   ⑱   59   ⑲   27
    + 18   + 87   + 46   + 33

⑳   19   ㉑   82   ㉒   51   ㉓   75
    − 12   − 37   − 36   − 16

What is the right sign? Draw <, >, or =.

㉔ 18 + 24 ◯ 30   ㉕ 19 − 7 ◯ 20

㉖   5 + 5 ◯ 10   ㉗ 8 + 4 ◯ 4 + 8

Add.

㉘   43   ㉙   26   ㉚   29   ㉛   16
        28   17   30   40
        62   30   43   29
    + 57   + 19   + 16   + 18

NOTE TO HOME
This test checks unit skills and concepts.

◆ **LESSON 115 Unit 3 Test**

Name _____

Solve these problems.

32 The soup costs $3. The hamburger costs $5. How much do they cost all together?

$ _____

$5

$3

33 The camera costs $75. The fan costs $49. How much do they cost all together?

$ _____

$75

$49

34 The radio costs $24. Ms. Duffy gave the salesperson $50. How much change should she get?

$ _____

$24

NOTE TO HOME
This test checks unit skills and concepts.

◆ **LESSON 115 Unit 3 Test**

What time is it?

③⑤ _____ : _____   ③⑥ _____ : _____   ③⑦ _____ : _____

③⑧ Color one third.   ③⑨ Color two thirds.

④⓪ There are 100 centimeters
in 1 meter. How many
centimeters are there in 4 meters? _____

NOTE TO HOME
This test checks unit skills and concepts.

LESSON 116

Name _____

Extending the Unit

Solve the cross-number puzzle.

Fill in the numbers.

```
┌─────┬─────┬─────┬─────┬─────┬─────┐
│ 1   │     │ 2   │█████│ 3   │█████│
│     │     │     │█████│     │█████│
├─────┼─────┼─────┼─────┼─────┼─────┤
│     │█████│ 4   │ 5   │     │█████│
│     │█████│     │     │     │█████│
├─────┼─────┼─────┼─────┼─────┼─────┤
│ 6   │ 7   │█████│     │█████│ 8   │
│     │     │█████│     │█████│     │
├─────┼─────┼─────┼─────┼─────┼─────┤
│█████│ 9   │█████│ 10  │     │     │
│█████│     │█████│     │     │     │
└─────┴─────┴─────┴─────┴─────┴─────┘
```

Across

1 94 + 18 = _____

4 15 minutes past 4 o'clock _____

6 36 − 17 = _____

8 _____ tens + 6 ones = 26

9 5:55 is about _____ o'clock

10 Number of centimeters in seven meters _____

Down

1 86 + 25 = _____

2 2 tens and 4 ones _____

3 69 − 34 = _____

5 69 + 58 = _____

7 42 + 54 = _____

8 43 − 23 = _____

10 26 − 19 = _____

NOTE TO HOME
Students complete a number puzzle.

◆ **LESSON 116 Extending the Unit**

Solve the cross-number puzzle.

Across

1 50 + 25 = _____

3 120 − 57 = _____

5 85 − 27 = _____

7 40 = _____ tens

8 68 + 38 = _____

10 1:10 is about
_____ o'clock

Down

1 63 − 56 = _____

2 _____ − 19 = 37

4 45 minutes
before 4 o'clock _____

5 43 + 13 = _____

6 7:55 is
5 minutes before _____

7 113 − 72 = _____

NOTE TO HOME
Students complete a number puzzle.

UNIT 4

Money and Multiplication

EXPLORING AND PROBLEM SOLVING

- collecting data

- algebra readiness

- adding and subtracting money

- three-digit addition and subtraction

- four-digit addition and subtraction

- division readiness

Bank tellers use math . . .

A bank teller keeps track of the money in your account. When you deposit or withdraw money, the teller uses addition and subtraction. A teller also uses skip counting or multiplication when counting money.

LESSON 117

Name _____

Introduction to Multiplication

Each triangle has three sides.
How many sides are there?

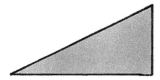

1 $3 + 3 + 3 + 3 + 3 =$ _____

2 $5 \times 3 =$ _____

Each car has four tires.
How many tires are there?

3 $4 + 4 + 4 + 4 =$ _____

4 $4 \times 4 =$ _____

Each box has six pencils.
How many pencils are there?

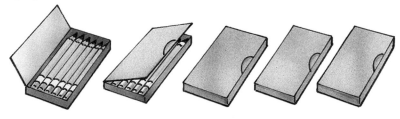

5 $6 + 6 + 6 + 6 + 6 =$ _____

6 $5 \times 6 =$ _____

NOTE TO HOME
Students are introduced to multiplication concepts.

◆ LESSON 117 Introduction to Multiplication

Skip count to find the missing numbers.
Use manipulatives if you need to.

7 | 2 | 4 | 6 | | 10 | | 14 | | | 20 |

8 $3 \times 2 =$ _____   **9** $5 \times 2 =$ _____

10 | 3 | 6 | | 12 | | 18 | | 24 | | 30 |

11 $2 \times 3 =$ _____   **12** $4 \times 3 =$ _____

13 | 5 | | 15 | | 25 | 30 | | 40 | | 50 |

14 $2 \times 5 =$ _____   **15** $8 \times 5 =$ _____

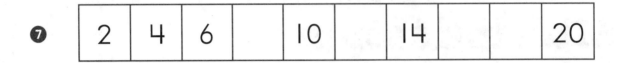

NOTE TO HOME
Students skip count.

LESSON 118

Name _____

Multiplication—Using Repeated Addition

Use these pictures to solve the problems.

3 + 3 + 3 + 3 + 3 + 3

1 6 × 3 = _____

6 + 6 + 6

2 3 × 6 = _____

     5
 +
      5
 +
     5
 +
 5

3 4 × 5 = _____

    4
+
    4
+
    4
+
    4
+
    4

4 5 × 4 = _____

NOTE TO HOME
Students use repeated addition to multiply.

◆ **LESSON 118** Multiplication—Using Repeated Addition

COOPERATIVE LEARNING

Solve these problems. Use the pictures.
Work in groups.

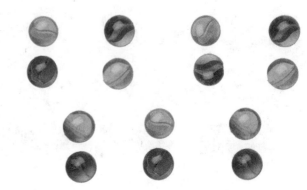

5 2 × 7 = _____

6 7 × 2 = _____

7 4 × 4 = _____

8 3 × 5 = _____

GAME

Play the "Add the Products" game.

THINKING STORY

Talk about the Thinking Story "Loretta the
Letter Carrier Chooses Sides."

NOTE TO HOME
Students practice multiplication and
play a multiplication game.

LESSON
119

Name _____

Multiplication—Finding Area

Count the squares.

1 The area of the foot is about _____
square units.

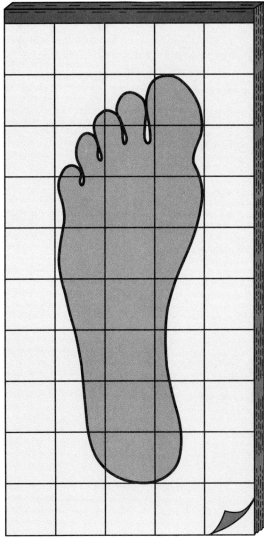

How did you count the squares?

2 The area of
the page is

_____ square units.

3 5 × 10 = _____

NOTE TO HOME
Students are introduced to the
concept of area.

◆ **LESSON 119 Multiplication—Finding Area**

Use the squares to solve these problems.

10 cm

10 cm

4 The area is

_____

square

centimeters.

5 10 × 10 =

_____

3 cm

5 cm

6 The area is _____ square
centimeters.

7 5 × 3 = _____

8 The area is _____ square centimeters.

9 3 × 14 = _____

NOTE TO HOME
Students use grids to find area.

LESSON
120

Name _____

Multiplication

Use these pictures to solve the problems.

1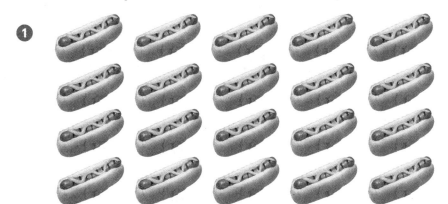

$5 + 5 + 5 + 5$

$4 \times 5 = $ _____

2

$4 + 4 + 4$

$3 \times 4 = $ _____

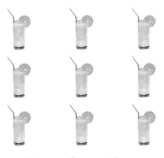

$3 + 3 + 3$

3 $3 \times 3 = $ _____

$2 + 2 + 2$

4 $3 \times 2 = $ _____

NOTE TO HOME
Students continue to explore repeated
addition to help them multiply.

◆ **LESSON 120 Multiplication**

Use these pictures to solve the problems.

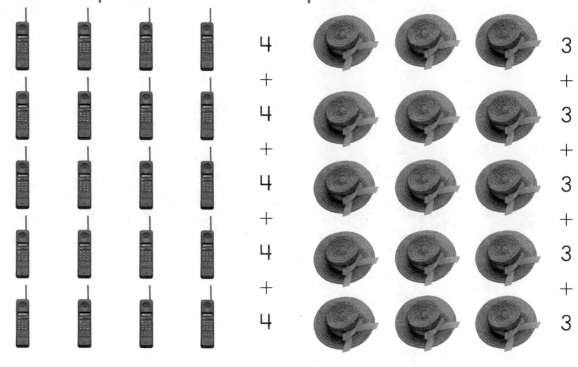

$$\begin{array}{c} 4 \\ + \\ 4 \\ + \\ 4 \\ + \\ 4 \\ + \\ 4 \end{array}$$

$$\begin{array}{c} 3 \\ + \\ 3 \\ + \\ 3 \\ + \\ 3 \\ + \\ 3 \end{array}$$

5 $5 \times 4 =$ _____

6 $5 \times 3 =$ _____

Solve this problem.

7 How many cookies do you think are on the tray?

_____

GAME

Play the "Multiplication Table" game.

NOTE TO HOME
Students practice multiplication and
solve word problems.

Name _____

Multiplication— Using Pictures

Use the pictures to solve the problems.

❶ 1 × 6 = _____

❷ 2 × 6 = _____

❸ 3 × 6 = _____

❹ 4 × 6 = _____

❺ 5 × 6 = _____

❻ 1 × 7 = _____

❼ 2 × 7 = _____

❽ 3 × 7 = _____

❾ 4 × 7 = _____

❿ 5 × 7 = _____

⓫ 1 × 8 = _____

⓬ 2 × 8 = _____

⓭ 3 × 8 = _____

⓮ 4 × 8 = _____

⓯ 5 × 8 = _____

NOTE TO HOME
Students use pictures to practice
multiplication facts.

◆ **LESSON 121 Multiplication—Using Pictures**

Use these pictures to solve the problems.

⑯ $1 \times 9 =$ _____

⑰ $2 \times 9 =$ _____

⑱ $3 \times 9 =$ _____

⑲ $4 \times 9 =$ _____

⑳ $5 \times 9 =$ _____

㉑ $1 \times 10 =$ _____

㉒ $2 \times 10 =$ _____

㉓ $3 \times 10 =$ _____

㉔ $4 \times 10 =$ _____

㉕ $5 \times 10 =$ _____

㉖ $9 \times 0 =$ _____

㉗ $3 \times 5 =$ _____

㉘ $5 \times 5 =$ _____

㉙ $3 \times 10 =$ _____

㉚ $5 \times 10 =$ _____

㉛ $5 \times 0 =$ _____

GAME

Play the "Add the Products" game.

NOTE TO HOME
Students practice multiplication facts.

Name _____

Applying Multiplication

Solve these
problems.

1 Each child has $6.
How much money
do they have all
together? $ _____

2 Corey read eight
pages every day
for seven days.
How many pages
did he read
that week? _____

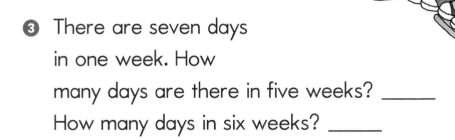

3 There are seven days
in one week. How
many days are there in five weeks? _____
How many days in six weeks? _____

4 There are four apartments in each building. How
many apartments are there in three buildings? _____

5 Lynette bought five action figures. Each figure
was $3. How much did Lynette pay in all? _____

NOTE TO HOME
Students practice solving realistic
multiplication problems.

◆ **LESSON 122 Applying Multiplication**

Fill in the missing numbers in each chart.

Sets of Five

6

0	I	2	3	4	5	6	7	8	9
0	5	10				30			45

Sets of Two

7

0	I	2	3	4	5	6	7	8	9
0	2	4							18

Sets of Three

8

0	I	2	3	4	5	6	7	8	9
	3	6							27

Use the charts to solve these problems.

9 $4 \times 5 = $ _____   **10** $8 \times 2 = $ _____   **11** $7 \times 3 = $ _____

Use your calculator to find each answer.
Write it in the space.

12 $4 \times 5 = $ _____

13 $8 \times 2 = $ _____

14 $7 \times 3 = $ _____

NOTE TO HOME
Students continue to explore multiplication.

Name _____

Multiplication

GAME

Play the "Multiplication Table" game.

Fill in the missing numbers.

1	0	2			8	10

2	0	5	10			25

3	0	3	6			15

FANTASTIC FACT

The longest sneezing attack lasted 978 days. If the sneezer sneezed only three times a day, how many sneezes would there be all together?

NOTE TO HOME
Students use a multiplication table.

◆ **LESSON 123 Multiplication**

Suzanne was selling bags of peanuts for 8¢ each. To help know how much money to collect, she made this chart.

Help Suzanne by completing the chart.

4

Bags	1	2	3	4	5	6	7	8		10
Price (in cents)	8		24				56		72	

5 What is the price of seven bags of peanuts? _____¢

Find the function rule.

6

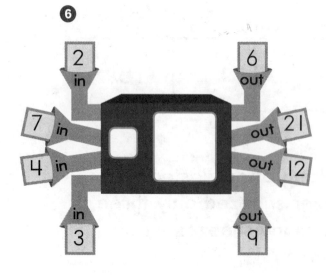

7

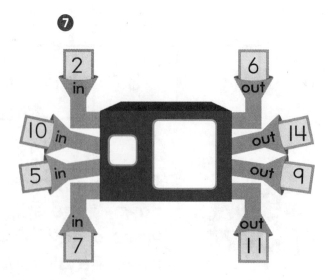

NOTE TO HOME
Students practice multiplication.

LESSON
124

Name _____

Analyzing Random Events

COOPERATIVE LEARNING Do the "Race Across the Room" activity.

Keep track of the colors.

First trial: I predict _____ will win.

Colors	Tallies	Totals

The winner was _____.

Second trial: I predict _____ will win.

Colors	Tallies	Totals

The winner was _____.

NOTE TO HOME
Students learn to collect and organize data.

◆ **LESSON 124 Analyzing Random Events**

CΦPERATIVE LEARNING Do the "Cube-Rolling" activity.

Keep track of the numbers you roll.

	Tallies	Totals	Class Totals
0			
1			
2			
3			
4			
5			

I am finding a class total for the number _____.

Keep sharp. Solve these problems.

1 5 × 10 = _____   **2** 4 × 6 = _____   **3** 8 × 3 = _____

4 2 × 9 = _____   **5** 7 × 3 = _____   **6** 2 × 2 = _____

One of every 50 Americans lives on a farm, and one of every 33 Americans says he or she doesn't eat candy.

NOTE TO HOME
Students use tally marks to collect data.

LESSON
125

Name _____

Predicting Results

Do the "Cube-Rolling" activity.

Keep track of the numbers you roll.

My number is _____.

	Tallies	Totals	Class Totals
5			
6			
7			
8			
9			
10			
11			
12			
13			
14			
15			

NOTE TO HOME
Students explore concepts of probability.

◆ **LESSON 125 Predicting Results**

Answer these questions before you play.

① What is the least difference you can roll? _____

② What is the greatest difference you can roll? _____

③ Which difference do you think will be rolled most often? _____

 Do the "Cube Rolling" activity, but subtract rather than add. Use these cubes:

Difference	Tallies	Totals	Class Totals

NOTE TO HOME
Students continue to explore concepts of probability.

LESSON 126

Name _____

Introducing Variability

How long is a used pencil?
Keep track of the centimeters.

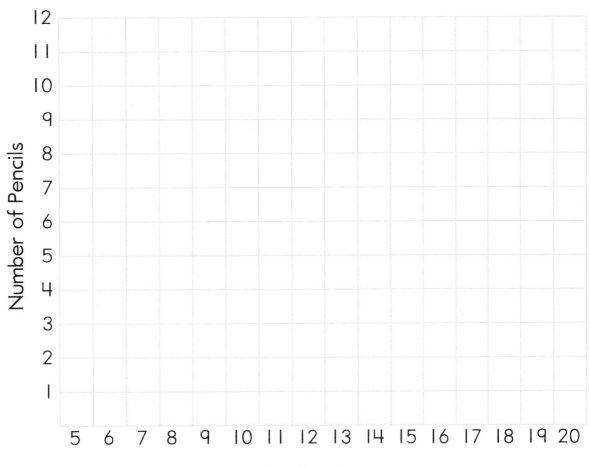

Number of Pencils (y-axis: 1–12)

Centimeters (x-axis: 5 6 7 8 9 10 11 12 13 14 15 16 17 18 19 20)

THINKING STORY

Talk about the Thinking Story
"Ms. Arthur's Budget, Part 1."

NOTE TO HOME
Students collect data and make a bar graph.

Unit 4   Lesson 126 • **283**

◆ **LESSON 126** Introducing Variability

How long is a new pencil?
Keep track of the centimeters.

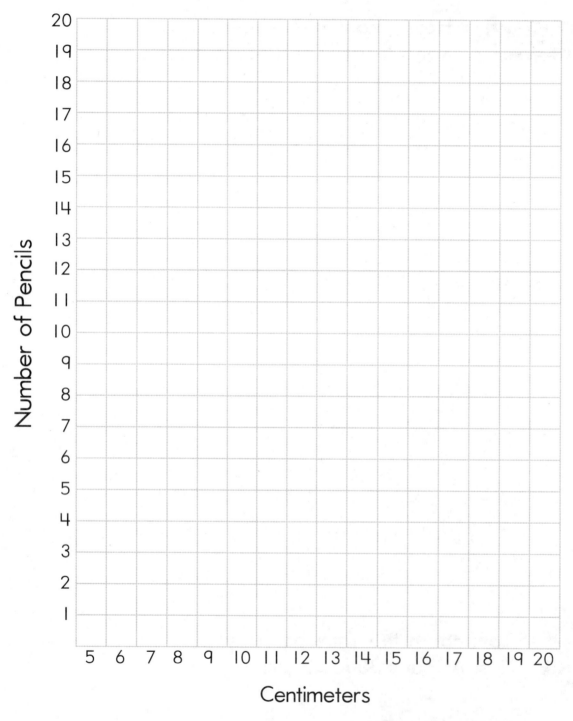

Number of Pencils

Centimeters

NOTE TO HOME
Students create, explore, and interpret
bar graphs.

LESSON
127

Name _____

Applying Multiplication

Work these problems.

There are five crayons in one box.

❶ How many crayons are there in two boxes?   _____

❷ How many crayons in three boxes?   _____

❸ How many crayons in four boxes?   _____

❹ How many crayons in five boxes?   _____

One pizza costs $4.

❺ How much do six pizzas cost? $_____

❻ How much do four pizzas cost? $_____

NOTE TO HOME
Students solve multiplication problems.

Unit 4   Lesson 127 • **285**

◆ **LESSON 127** Applying Multiplication

Use counters to create and solve these multiplication situations. Check to be sure your answers make sense.

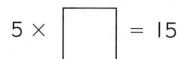

7 Nancy wants to buy 15 balloons. They come five to a box. How many boxes must she buy?

$$5 \times \boxed{} = 15$$

8 Miriam needs to put 28 pictures in her album. She wants to put four pictures on each page. How many pages will she need?

$$4 \times \boxed{} = 28$$

9 Courtney wants to earn $40. She can make $5 a week. How many weeks will it take her?

$$5 \times \boxed{} = 40$$

Solve these problems.

10 $4 \times \boxed{} = 8$ **11** $5 \times \boxed{} = 15$

12 $\boxed{} \times 4 = 8$ **13** $5 \times \boxed{} = 20$

14 $10 \times \boxed{} = 50$ **15** $5 \times \boxed{} = 25$

286 • Money and Multiplication

NOTE TO HOME
Students solve multiplication problems with missing factors.

LESSON
128

Name _____

Introducing Division

 Do the "Missing Factor Puzzle" activity.

Solve these problems.

1 I paid 21¢ for seven candles.

How much would one candle cost? _____ ¢

Sun	Mon	Tues	Wed	Thur	Fri	Sat
1	2	3	4	5	6	7
8	9	10	11	12	13	14
15	16	17	18	19	20	21
22	23	24	25	26	27	28
29	30	31				

There are seven days in one week.

2 How many weeks are there in 14 days? _____

3 How many weeks are there in 35 days? _____

4 How many weeks are there in 49 days? _____

5 How many weeks are there in 28 days? _____

 NOTE TO HOME
Students play a game and begin to learn about division.

◆ **LESSON 128** Introducing Division

COOPERATIVE LEARNING Use coins or counters to act these out in a group.

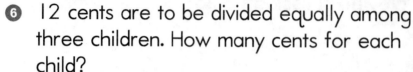

Solve these problems.

6 12 cents are to be divided equally among three children. How many cents for each child?

$$12 \div 3 = \underline{}$$

7 24 cents are to be divided equally among four children. How many cents for each child?

$$24 \div 4 = \underline{}$$

8 32 cents are to be divided equally among eight children. How many cents for each child?

$$32 \div 8 = \underline{}$$

9 15 cents are to be divided equally among three cups. How many cents in each cup?

$$15 \div 3 = \underline{}$$

NOTE TO HOME
Students use coins or counters to learn about division.

Name _____

Division and Multiplication

Solve these problems.

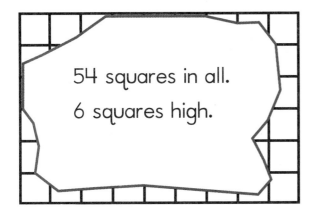

54 squares in all.

6 squares high.

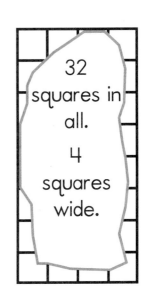

32 squares in all.

4 squares wide.

① How many squares long?

_____ squares long

② How many squares high?

_____ squares high

Sharpen your skills. Remember the doubles!

③ $1 + 1 =$ _____

④ $2 + 2 =$ _____

⑤ $3 + 3 =$ _____

⑥ $4 + 4 =$ _____

⑦ $5 + 5 =$ _____

⑧ $6 + 6 =$ _____

⑨ $7 + 7 =$ _____

⑩ $8 + 8 =$ _____

⑪ $9 + 9 =$ _____

⑫ $10 + 10 =$ _____

NOTE TO HOME
Students explore division and
review adding doubles.

◆ **LESSON 129** Division and Multiplication

Use play money to help solve these problems. Check to be sure your answers make sense.

⑬ Paul sells baskets of strawberries for $3 a basket. He made this chart to help him know how much to collect. Help Paul by completing the chart.

Number of baskets	1	2	3	4	5	6	7	8	9	10
Price (dollars)	3	6	9	12						

Use the chart to answer these questions.

⑭ Sara bought five baskets. What did she pay?

$$3 \times 5 = \boxed{}$$

⑮ Megan paid $24. How many did she buy?

$$\boxed{} \times 3 = 24$$

⑯ Raulito paid $9. How many did he buy?

$$\boxed{} \times 3 = 9$$

⑰ Late in the season Paul raised his prices. Then he sold five baskets of strawberries for $20. What was the new price?_____

$$5 \times \boxed{} = 20$$

290 · Money and Multiplication

NOTE TO HOME
Students solve word problems.

Copyright © SRA/McGraw-Hill

UNIT
4

Name _____

Mid-Unit Review

Solve these problems. Use the pictures.

1

2

$7 \times 2 = $ _____ $3 \times 8 = $ _____

Use the squares to solve these problems.

3

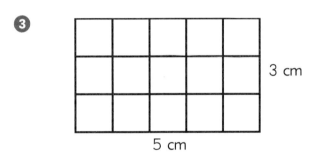

3 cm

5 cm

The area is _____ square centimeters.

4

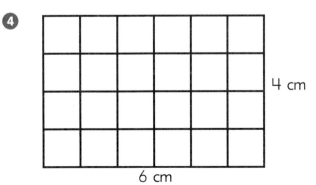

4 cm

6 cm

The area is _____ square centimeters.

NOTE TO HOME
Students review unit skills and concepts.

◆ **UNIT 4 Mid-Unit Review**

5 Fill in the missing numbers in the chart.

0	1	2	3	4	5	6	7	8	9
0	4	8			20			32	36

Use the chart above to solve these problems.

6 3 × 4 = _____   **7** 4 × 7 = _____

8 4 × 9 = _____

9 José made the following chart to help him know how much to charge for balloons. Help José by completing the chart.

Number of balloons	1	2	3	4	5	6	7	8	9	10
Price (cents)	6		18		30			48		60

10 What is the price of nine balloons? _____

11 Kelly bought eight balloons.
She gave José 50¢.
How much did she get back? _____

12 Daniel bought one balloon for his sister, two for his mother, and one for his aunt.
How much did he pay? _____

NOTE TO HOME
Students review unit skills and concepts.

Name _____

Days of the Week

Fill in the missing days.

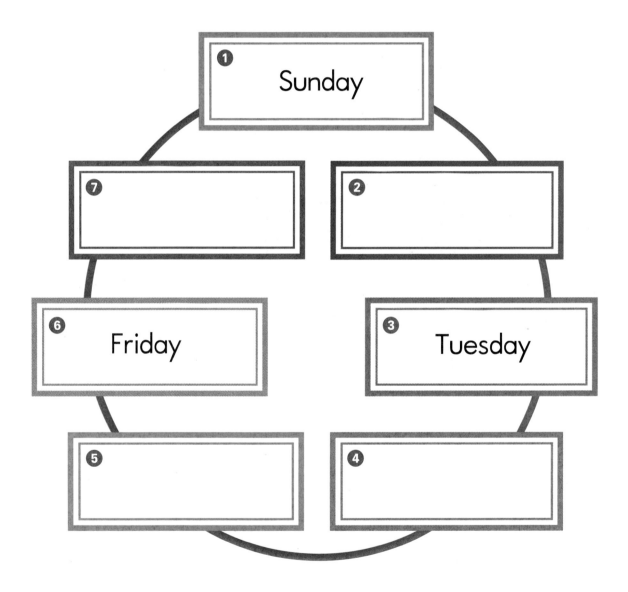

1. Sunday

7.

2.

6. Friday

3. Tuesday

5.

4.

NOTE TO HOME
Students practice ordering the days of the week.

◆ **LESSON 130 Days of the Week**

Draw a ring around the day it is today.

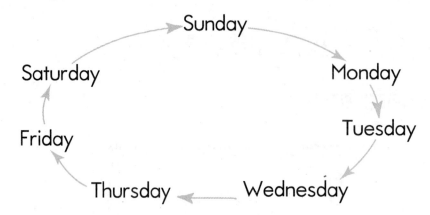

Use today to complete the chart. Write
the day it was and the day it will be.

Number of Days	Day It Was	Day It Will Be
1	⑧	⑨
3	⑩	⑪
6	⑫	⑬
7	⑭	⑮
8	⑯	⑰
14	⑱	⑲
21	⑳	㉑
69	㉒	㉓
70	㉔	㉕
71	㉖	㉗

NOTE TO HOME
Students learn to identify days of the
week by using multiples.

LESSON 131

Name _____

Telling Time

The time now is 4:00 P.M.

Complete the chart. Show the time it was and the time it will be.

Number of Hours	Time It Was	Time It Will Be
1	3:00 P.M.	5:00 P.M.
2	❶	❷
4	❸	❹
8	❺	❻
12	❼	❽
24	❾	❿
36	⓫	⓬
48	⓭	⓮
72	⓯	⓰
73	⓱	⓲

NOTE TO HOME
Students learn to identify the time after a specific number of hours have passed.

◆ **LESSON 131 Telling Time**

19 Mrs. Fontana gave her class an assignment on Friday and said it must be finished in eight days.

What day of the week will that be? _____

20 What's wrong with Mrs. Fontana's assignment? _____

_____

 How many seconds does it take? First estimate. Write in the chart below. Then work in small groups to check.

21 Count to 50   22 Count to 25

23 Say the sentence at the bottom of the page clearly.

24 Say the sentence at the bottom of this page clearly twice.

Task	Estimate (in seconds)	Measure (in seconds)
21		
22		
23		
24		

 She sells sea shells by the seashore.

 NOTE TO HOME
Students practice solving problems involving elapsed time.

296 • Money and Multiplication

LESSON
132

Name _____

Number Sentences

Write three number sentences that give
the number shown as the answer.

10 ❶ $\underline{5 + 3 + 6 - 4 = 10}$

❷ _____

❸ _____

8 ❹ _____

❺ _____

❻ _____

5 ❼ _____

❽ _____

❾ _____

Play the "Harder What's the Problem?" game.

NOTE TO HOME
Students learn to create different number
sequences with the same answer.

◆ **LESSON 132 Number Sentences**

Write a number sentence for each problem. Then solve the problem.

10 Mary earned $5 on Monday, $7 on Tuesday, and $4 on Wednesday. How many dollars did she earn in the three days? $_____

11 Samantha had nine marbles. She bought two more. Then she gave three away. Then she got three more. How many marbles does Samantha have now? _____

12 John earned $3 a day for seven days. How many dollars has he earned? $_____

13 There were 20 apples on the tree. Abby picked three apples a day for five days. One apple fell off the tree. How many apples are on the tree? _____

NOTE TO HOME
Students solve word problems.

LESSON
133

Name _____

Grouping by Tens

Solve these problems. Use shortcuts if you can.

1 1 + 3 + 7 + 9 = _____

2 6 + 7 + 4 = _____

3 4 + 6 + 7 + 3 + 5 + 5 + 9 + 1 = _____

4 1 + 2 + 3 + 4 + 5 + 6 + 7 + 8 + 9 = _____

5 1 + 3 + 5 + 7 + 9 = _____

6 6 + 7 + 4 + 3 = _____

7 8 + 2 + 9 + 1 + 7 + 3 + 6 + 4 + 10 = _____

8 4 + 6 + 2 + 8 + 3 + 7 = _____

9 7 + 3 + 1 + 9 + 5 + 5 + 3 = _____

10 5 + 5 + 6 + 4 + 1 + 9 + 7 = _____

Ring one problem. In your Math Journal tell what shortcuts you used.

NOTE TO HOME
Students use patterns to add mentally.

◆ **LESSON 133 Grouping by Tens**

Solve these problems. Use mental math where
you can. Many are easier than they look.

11 4 + 1 + 3 + 2 + 5 + 0 + 2 + 3 = _____

12 10 + 9 + 8 + 2 + 1 + 10 = _____

13 2 + 4 + 6 + 8 + 10 = _____

14 20 + 40 + 60 + 80 + 100 = _____

15 21 + 19 + 32 + 18 = _____

16 3 × 3 × 3 = _____

17 2 × 2 × 2 × 2 = _____

18 9 + 1 + 10 + 19 + 1 + 30 = _____

19 42 + 8 + 5 + 6 + 5 + 4 = _____

20 Tell an easy way to solve one of
these problems.

**THINKING
STORY**

Talk about the Thinking Story
"Ms. Arthur's Budget, Part 2."

NOTE TO HOME
Students use mental math.

Name _____

Multiplication and Division

Find the function rules.

1

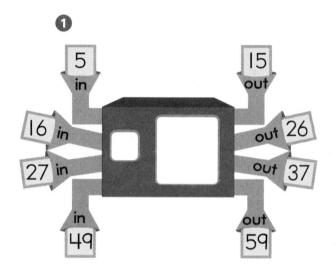

2

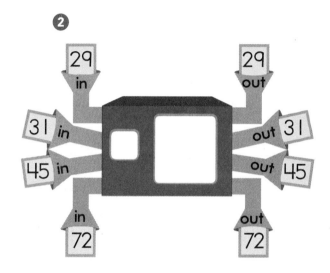

3

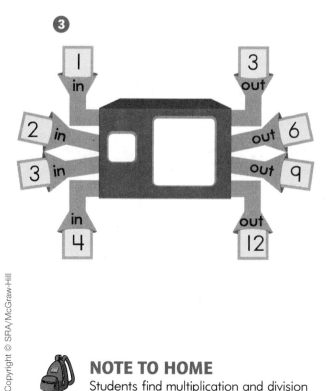

4

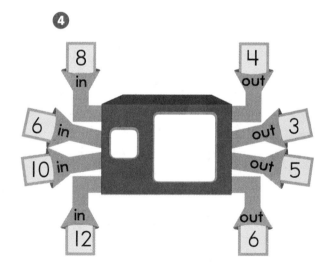

NOTE TO HOME
Students find multiplication and division
function rules.

◆ **LESSON 134 Multiplication and Division**

Find the function rules. Then fill in the missing numbers.

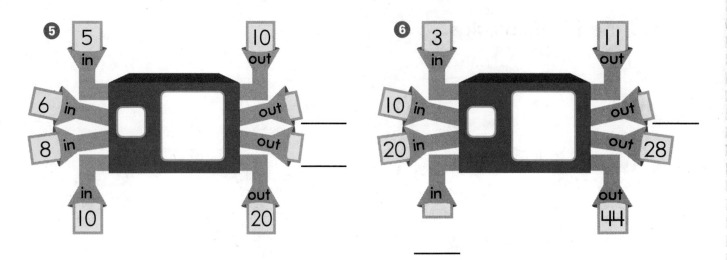

Make up your own function rule problems.
Challenge a friend to solve them.

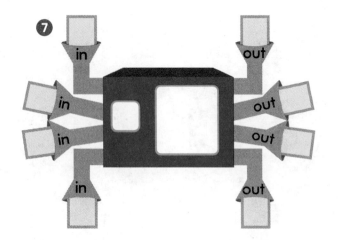

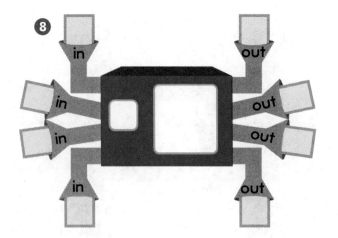

NOTE TO HOME
Students find and create function rules.

Name _____

Mixed Operations

1. Kevin was making hard function problems. His rule is $+9 - 4$. Fill in the missing numbers.

2. Write what's hard about Kevin's problem. _____
_____

3. Write what's easy about Kevin's problem. _____
_____

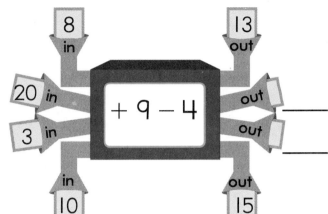

4. Lorena was also trying to make hard function problems. Here's her problem. The rule is $\times 3 - 1$. Fill in the missing numbers.

5. Write what's hard about Lorena's problem. _____
_____

6. Write what's easy about Lorena's problem. _____
_____

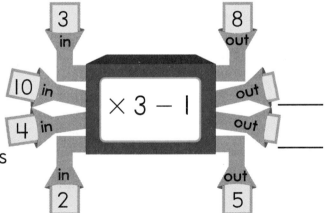

NOTE TO HOME
Students practice mixed operation function rules.

◆ **LESSON 135 Mixed Operations**

C⬤OPERATIVE LEARNING Work with a partner to solve these problems. They are harder than they look.

7

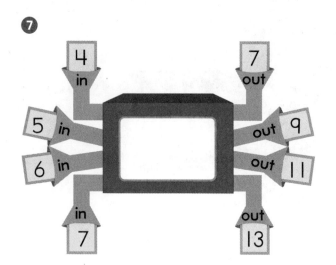

8

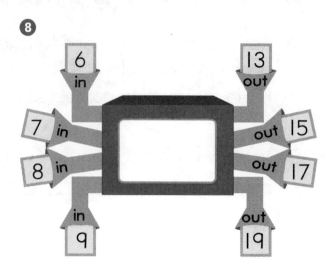

Make up your own function rule problems. Challenge a friend to solve them.

9

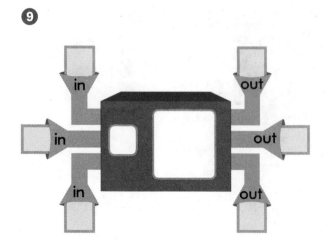

10

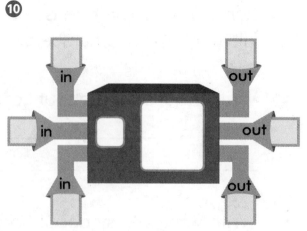

304 • Money and Multiplication

NOTE TO HOME
Students solve mixed operation function rules.

Name _____

More Mixed Operations

1 Matt charges $3 per hour for mowing lawns, plus $1 to cover the cost of his travel.

Complete the chart to show how much Matt should collect.

Matt's Lawn Mowing Service Price Chart								
Hours	1	2	3	4	5	6	7	8
Charge (dollars)	4	7	10					

Allison also mows lawns. She estimates how long a job will take. Then she charges a fixed price for her service.

2 Which method of charging is fairer, Matt's or Allison's? Write why you think so. _____

_____

_____

NOTE TO HOME
Students complete function charts.

◆ **LESSON 136 More Mixed Operations**

Kenji was busy making hard function problems. Use a calculator to see why they really aren't so hard. Then write an easy rule for each problem.

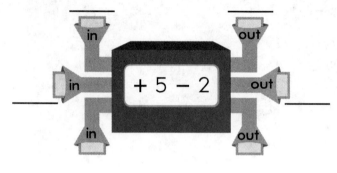

+ 5 − 2

❸ The easy rule is
_____.

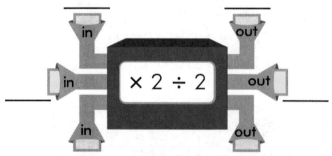

× 2 ÷ 2

❹ The easy rule is
_____.

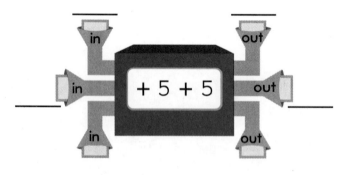

+ 5 + 5

❺ The easy rule is
_____.

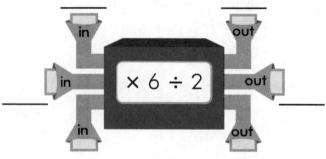

× 6 ÷ 2

❻ The easy rule is
_____.

NOTE TO HOME
Students find function rules.

LESSON
137

Name _____

Keeping Sharp

$$\begin{array}{r} \text{I} \\ 27 \\ + 65 \\ \hline 2 \end{array}$$

$$\begin{array}{r} \text{I} \\ 27 \\ + 65 \\ \hline 92 \end{array}$$

Solve.

1 54 + 35 = _____

2 65 + 28 = _____

3 35 + 35 = _____

4 24 + 24 = _____

5 82 + 9 = _____

6 26 + 27 = _____

7 25 + 29 = _____

8 43 + 37 = _____

9 99 + 34 = _____

10 32 + 27 = _____

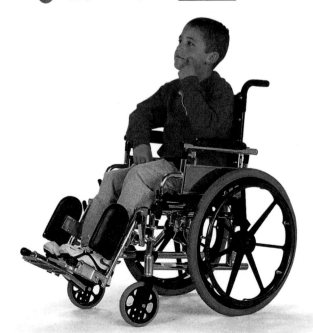

NOTE TO HOME
Students review two-digit addition.

Unit 4   Lesson 137 • **307**

◆ **LESSON 137 Keeping Sharp**

$$\begin{array}{r} \overset{3\ 13}{\cancel{43}} \\ -\ 25 \\ \hline \end{array}$$

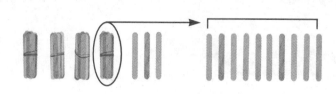

$$\begin{array}{r} \overset{3\ 13}{\cancel{43}} \\ -\ 25 \\ \hline 18 \end{array}$$

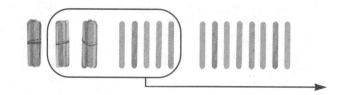

Solve.

11 $82 - 75 =$ _____

12 $23 - 23 =$ _____

13 $45 - 17 =$ _____

14 $62 - 25 =$ _____

15 $50 - 25 =$ _____

16 $54 - 29 =$ _____

17 $65 - 18 =$ _____

18 $65 - 19 =$ _____

19 $56 - 29 =$ _____

20 $83 - 27 =$ _____

21 $46 - 23 =$ _____

22 $97 - 34 =$ _____

23 $62 - 32 =$ _____

24 $50 - 35 =$ _____

25 $93 - 86 =$ _____

26 $27 - 8 =$ _____

NOTE TO HOME
Students review two-digit subtraction.

LESSON
138

Name _____

Counting Through 1000

Write how many cookies are in each group.

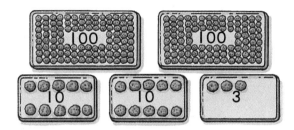

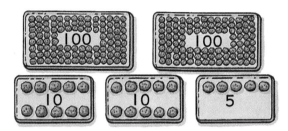

1 _____

2 _____

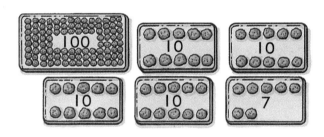

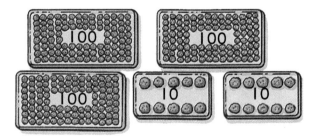

3 _____

4 _____

GAME

Play the "Harder Counting and
Writing Numbers" game.

NOTE TO HOME
Students learn to count hundreds, tens, and ones.

Unit 4   Lesson 138 • **309**

◆ **LESSON 138 Counting Through 1000**

Draw pictures to show the number of cookies. Instead of drawing 100 cookies on some sheets, you may write 100 like this.

100

5 253 cookies

6 307 cookies

What is the right sign? Draw <, >, or =.

7 635 ◯ 792   **8** 999 ◯ 909

Fill in the missing numbers.

9

132	133		135			138

10

993	994			997		999

NOTE TO HOME
Students show and count numbers from 0–1000.

LESSON
139

Name _____

Numbers Through 1000

Count up or count down. Fill in the missing numbers.

1 | 97 | 98 | | | | 102 | | 104 |

2 | 706 | 707 | | | | | 712 | 713 |

3 | 843 | 842 | 841 | | | 838 | | 836 |

4 | 999 | 998 | 997 | | | | | 992 |

5 | 413 | 412 | 411 | | | | | 406 |

COOPERATIVE LEARNING   Do the "How Many Sticks?" activity.

6 Guess _____

7 First estimate _____

8 Last estimate _____

NOTE TO HOME
Students practice counting from 0–1000.

◆ **LESSON 139 Numbers Through 1000**

Check your math skills.

⑨ 2 + 3 = _____   ⑩ 2 + 4 = _____

⑪ 3 + 2 = _____   ⑫ 13 − 7 = _____

⑬ 5 − 1 = _____   ⑭ 8 + 2 = _____

⑮ 6 + 2 = _____   ⑯ 5 + 1 = _____

⑰ 7 − 3 = _____   ⑱ 8 − 3 = _____

⑲ 10 + 5 = _____

⑳ 3 + 7 = _____

㉑ 6 + 6 = _____

㉒ 9 − 3 = _____

Number correct ☐

 NOTE TO HOME
Students review addition and subtraction skills.

LESSON
140

Name _____

Introducing Three-Digit Addition

9 tens and 3 tens = 1 hundred and 2 tens

Write the correct number less than ten in each blank.

1 7 and 6 = _____ tens and _____

2 7 tens and 6 tens = _____ hundreds and _____ tens

3 5 and 7 = _____ tens and _____

4 5 tens and 7 tens = _____ hundreds and _____ tens

5 3 and 8 = _____ tens and _____

6 3 tens and 8 tens = _____ hundreds and _____ tens

7 6 and 9 = _____ tens and _____

8 6 tens and 9 tens = _____ hundreds and _____ tens

NOTE TO HOME
Students regroup tens and hundreds.

◆ **LESSON 140 Introducing Three-Digit Addition**

Write the correct number less than ten in each box.

tens
⬜

9   7
    + 6

⬜

tens
⬜

10   5
    + 8

⬜

tens
⬜

11   8
    + 8

⬜

hundreds
⬜

12   7 tens
    + 6 tens

⬜ tens

hundreds
⬜

13   5 tens
    + 8 tens

⬜ tens

hundreds
⬜

14   9 tens
    + 7 tens

⬜ tens

hundreds
⬜

15   3 tens
    + 8 tens

⬜ tens

tens
⬜

16   8
    + 3

⬜

NOTE TO HOME
Students prepare for adding three-digit
numbers with regrouping.

LESSON 141

Name _____

Three-Digit Addition

Use sticks to add.

325 + 289 = __?__   Write what you did.

$$
\begin{array}{r}
325 \\
+\ 289 \\
\hline
\end{array}
$$

$$
\begin{array}{r}
\overset{1}{3}25 \\
+\ 289 \\
\hline
4
\end{array}
$$

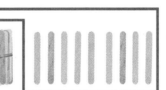

$$
\begin{array}{r}
\overset{1\,1}{3}25 \\
+\ 289 \\
\hline
14
\end{array}
$$

$$
\begin{array}{r}
\overset{1\,1}{3}25 \\
+\ 289 \\
\hline
614
\end{array}
$$

 NOTE TO HOME
Students learn how to use models to help them add three-digit numbers.

Unit 4   Lesson 141 • **315**

◆ **LESSON 141 Three-Digit Addition**

Solve these problems.

 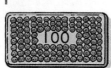

① How many cookies? _____

253
+ 325

$355
+ 264

② How much money? $ _____

Draw pictures or use manipulatives
to add. Record your answer.

③	103	④	$271	⑤	525
	+ 457		+ 660		+ 347

GAME

Play the "Rummage Sale" game.

NOTE TO HOME
Students use models to add three-digit numbers.

◆ **LESSON 141 Three-Digit Addition** Name _____

Rewrite and add.

229	2 hundreds 2 tens and 9
+163	1 hundred 6 tens and 3
392	3 hundreds 8 tens and 12
	or
	3 hundreds 9 tens and 2

Solve.

6   347   _____ hundreds _____ tens and _____
     + 572   + _____ hundreds _____ tens and _____

7   273   _____ hundreds _____ tens and _____
     + 419   + _____ hundreds _____ ten and _____

8   623   _____ hundreds _____ tens and _____
     + 189   + _____ hundred _____ tens and _____

NOTE TO HOME
Students add by expanded counting.

◆ **LESSON 141 Three-Digit Addition**

Add.

9
$$\begin{array}{r} \overset{1}{}327 \\ + 269 \\ \hline 596 \end{array}$$

10
$$\begin{array}{r} 700 \\ + 800 \\ \hline \end{array}$$

11
$$\begin{array}{r} 205 \\ + 304 \\ \hline \end{array}$$

12
$$\begin{array}{r} 200 \\ + 500 \\ \hline \end{array}$$

13
$$\begin{array}{r} 432 \\ + 385 \\ \hline \end{array}$$

14
$$\begin{array}{r} 689 \\ + 219 \\ \hline \end{array}$$

15
$$\begin{array}{r} 434 \\ + 656 \\ \hline \end{array}$$

16
$$\begin{array}{r} 287 \\ + 342 \\ \hline \end{array}$$

17
$$\begin{array}{r} 250 \\ + 250 \\ \hline \end{array}$$

18
$$\begin{array}{r} 100 \\ + 300 \\ \hline \end{array}$$

19
$$\begin{array}{r} 100 \\ + 250 \\ \hline \end{array}$$

20
$$\begin{array}{r} 507 \\ + 103 \\ \hline \end{array}$$

NOTE TO HOME
Students add three-digit numbers with and without regrouping.

LESSON
142

Name _____

More Three-Digit Addition

Add.

①
```
   432
 + 158
```

②
```
   276
 + 395
```

③
```
   403
 + 608
```

④
```
   302
 + 708
```

⑤
```
   536
 + 492
```

⑥
```
   507
 + 394
```

⑦
```
   574
 + 687
```

⑧
```
   325
 + 244
```

⑨
```
   345
 + 655
```

⑩
```
   625
 + 264
```

⑪
```
   493
 + 388
```

⑫
```
   449
 + 106
```

THINKING STORY

Talk about the Thinking Story "Manolita Changes Things."

NOTE TO HOME
Students add three-digit numbers.

◆ **LESSON 142 More Three-Digit Addition**

Add.

⑬   547
   + 382

⑭   659
   + 147

⑮   506
   + 384

⑯   521
   + 87

⑰   43
   + 812

⑱   342
   + 9

⑲   8
   + 642

⑳   125
   + 125

㉑   250
   + 250

㉒   600
   + 300

㉓   704
   + 200

㉔   704
   + 20

FANTASTIC FACT

In one season professional football teams use 300 miles of adhesive tape.

NOTE TO HOME
Students add one-, two-, and three-digit numbers.

LESSON 143

Name _____

Three-Digit Subtraction

Rewrite to show more tens.

321 = __2__ hundreds, __12__ tens, and __1__

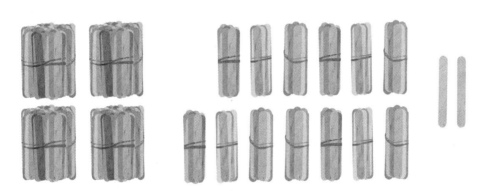

1 532 = _____ hundreds, _____ tens, and _____

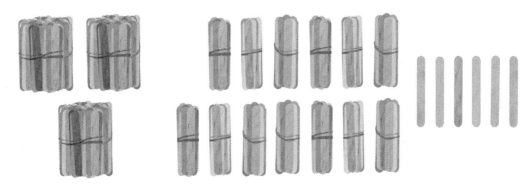

2 436 = _____ hundreds, _____ tens, and _____

NOTE TO HOME
Students regroup hundreds to tens.

◆ LESSON 143 Three-Digit Subtraction

Subtract.

$$350 - 70 = \underline{\quad ? \quad}$$

$$\begin{array}{r} 350 \\ -\ \ 70 \\ \hline \end{array}$$

I can't take
7 tens from
5 tens.

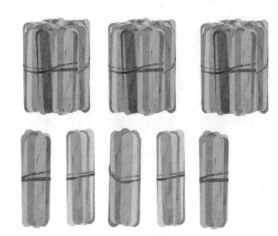

I can undo
a bundle
of one
hundred.

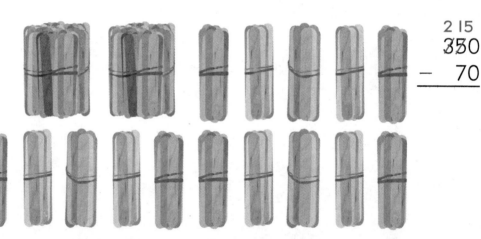

$$\begin{array}{r} {}^{2\ 15} \\ 3\!\!\!/5\!\!\!/0 \\ -\ \ 70 \\ \hline \end{array}$$

Now I
can take
away 7
tens.

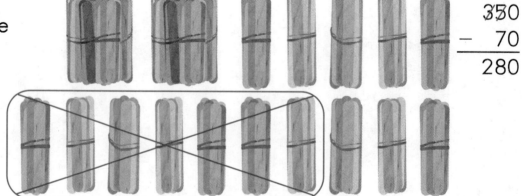

$$\begin{array}{r} {}^{2\ 15} \\ 3\!\!\!/5\!\!\!/0 \\ -\ \ 70 \\ \hline 280 \end{array}$$

NOTE TO HOME
Students learn how to model subtraction by
regrouping sticks.

◆ LESSON 143 Three-Digit Subtraction

Subtract.

You may rewrite the numbers when it helps you.

3

$$15 - 7$$ $$150 - 70$$

4

$$12 - 5$$ $$120 - 50$$

5

$$35 - 7$$ $$350 - 70$$

6

$$62 - 5$$ $$620 - 50$$

7

$$13 - 9$$ $$130 - 90$$

8

$$14 - 8$$ $$140 - 80$$

9

$$43 - 9$$ $$430 - 90$$

10

$$94 - 8$$ $$940 - 80$$

NOTE TO HOME
Students practice regrouping.

◆ **LESSON 143 Three-Digit Subtraction**

Subtract.

⑪   14   ⑫   140   ⑬   11   ⑭   110
    − 6   − 60   − 9   − 90

⑮   52   ⑯   520   ⑰   37   ⑱   370
    − 6   − 60   − 4   − 40

⑲   12   ⑳   120   ㉑   49   ㉒   490
    − 9   − 90   − 4   − 40

㉓   83   ㉔   830   ㉕   65   ㉖   650
    − 6   − 60   − 7   − 70

NOTE TO HOME
Students use patterns to subtract three-digit numbers.

LESSON 144

Name _____

More Three-Digit Subtraction

Use play money to subtract.

Write what you did.

$626 - 252 = \underline{\quad ? \quad}$

$$\begin{array}{r} 626 \\ -\ 252 \\ \hline \end{array}$$

$$\begin{array}{r} {\scriptstyle 5\ 12} \\ 6\llap{/}26 \\ -\ 252 \\ \hline \end{array}$$

$$\begin{array}{r} {\scriptstyle 5\ 12} \\ 6\llap{/}26 \\ -\ 252 \\ \hline 374 \end{array}$$

NOTE TO HOME
Students use play money to learn how to subtract with regrouping.

◆ **LESSON 144** More Three-Digit Subtraction

Solve these problems. Use
play money to help.

1 Mrs. Mazingo had $357 in the bank.
She took out $165. How many dollars
does she have in the bank now? _____

2 Mr. Ebert had $275 in his bank account.
Then he put in $156. How many dollars
does he have in the bank now? _____

3 The girls' basketball team needs $500 to
travel to the finals. So far, they have earned
$250. How many more dollars do they need? _____

4 Mr. Culyer drove 257 miles to visit his sister.
About how many miles will the round trip be? _____

326 • Money and Multiplication

LESSON 145

Name _____

Practicing Three-Digit Subtraction

Subtract. The first one has been done for you.

1.
$$
\begin{array}{r}
\overset{6\ 13}{4\cancel{7}\cancel{3}} \\
-218 \\
\hline
255
\end{array}
$$

2.
$$
\begin{array}{r}
675 \\
-384 \\
\hline
\end{array}
$$

3.
$$
\begin{array}{r}
582 \\
-272 \\
\hline
\end{array}
$$

4.
$$
\begin{array}{r}
504 \\
-217 \\
\hline
\end{array}
$$

5.
$$
\begin{array}{r}
608 \\
-319 \\
\hline
\end{array}
$$

6.
$$
\begin{array}{r}
705 \\
-204 \\
\hline
\end{array}
$$

7.
$$
\begin{array}{r}
600 \\
-357 \\
\hline
\end{array}
$$

8.
$$
\begin{array}{r}
200 \\
-169 \\
\hline
\end{array}
$$

9.
$$
\begin{array}{r}
410 \\
-328 \\
\hline
\end{array}
$$

10.
$$
\begin{array}{r}
892 \\
-538 \\
\hline
\end{array}
$$

11.
$$
\begin{array}{r}
479 \\
-265 \\
\hline
\end{array}
$$

12.
$$
\begin{array}{r}
503 \\
-247 \\
\hline
\end{array}
$$

NOTE TO HOME
Students subtract three-digit numbers with and without regrouping.

◆ **LESSON 145 Practicing Three-Digit Subtraction**

Subtract.

⑬
```
  7 15 13
  8̶6̶3̶
- 398
─────
  465
```

⑭
```
  408
- 372
─────
```

⑮
```
  604
- 257
─────
```

⑯
```
  621
- 358
─────
```

⑰
```
  429
- 275
─────
```

⑱
```
  599
- 389
─────
```

⑲
```
  212
-  87
─────
```

⑳
```
  300
-  25
─────
```

㉑
```
  516
- 248
─────
```

㉒
```
  250
-  25
─────
```

㉓
```
  397
- 209
─────
```

When the Apollo astronauts walked on the moon, they left footprints that will last for ten million years.

328 • Money and Multiplication

NOTE TO HOME
Students subtract from three-digit numbers.

Name _____

Three-Digit Addition and Subtraction

Solve these problems. Watch the signs.

①
```
   28
 + 37
```

②
```
   97
 + 84
```

③
```
   85
 - 26
```

④
```
   215
 + 346
```

⑤
```
   397
 + 284
```

⑥
```
   571
 - 222
```

⑦
```
   402
 - 204
```

⑧
```
   674
 +  88
```

⑨
```
   417
 - 205
```

⑩
```
   1000
 -  250
```

⑪
```
   317
 + 239
```

⑫
```
   412
 - 195
```

NOTE TO HOME
Students practice mixed three-digit addition and
three-digit subtraction problems.

◆ LESSON 146 Three-Digit Addition and Subtraction

Every year Big City has a 15-mile marathon.
Records of the marathon are kept. Last year
these were the records.

	Total Number	Male	Female	12–17	18–39	40–65	66+
Start	745	347	398	128	439	165	13
Finish	525	239	286	88	335	99	3

Answer these questions. If you don't have
enough information, write an X.

⑬ How many people finished the race? _____

⑭ How many didn't finish? _____

⑮ How many people younger than 40 finished? _____

⑯ How many 18-year-old boys finished the race? _____

⑰ How many males didn't finish? _____

⑱ How many females younger than 40 finished? _____

Write your own problems. Challenge a friend
to solve them.

NOTE TO HOME
Students practice addition, subtraction, and
reading charts.

LESSON **147**

Name _____

Three-Digit Practice

Look at this example of how to add.

Step 1	Step 2	Step 3
1	1 1	1 1
257	257	257
+375	+375	+375
2	3 2	6 3 2

Look at this example of how to subtract.

Step 1	Step 2	Step 3
	15	15
5 15	2 5 15	2 5 15
3 6 5	3 6 5	3 6 5
−1 7 9	−1 7 9	−1 7 9
6	8 6	1 8 6

Look at this example of how to subtract.

Step 1	Step 2
69 18	69 18
7 0 8	7 0 8
−4 6 9	−4 6 9
	2 3 9

NOTE TO HOME
Students review how to add and subtract three-digit numbers with regrouping.

◆ **LESSON 147 Three-Digit Practice**

Solve these problems. Watch the signs.

1   69
     + 58

2   173
     − 94

3   289
     + 347

4   620
     − 438

5   200
     − 83

6   547
     + 123

7   250
     + 750

8   482
     − 303

9   487
     − 99

10   487
     + 99

11   487
     + 101

12   343
     − 218

13   527
     + 109

14   175
     − 69

15   398
     − 157

Play the "Harder Rummage Sale" game.

NOTE TO HOME
Students review three digit addition and subtraction.

LESSON
148

Name _____

Adding and Subtracting Money

GAME   Play the "Make a $10 Bill" game.

Write how much.

① ___100___ cents      ② _____ cents

③ _____ cents      ④ _____ cents

⑤ _____ cents      ⑥ _____ cents

⑦ 150 cents = $ __1.50__   ⑧ $1.25 = _____ cents

⑨ 175 cents = $ ___.___   ⑩ $ 2.38 = _____ cents

⑪ 96 cents = $ ___.___   ⑫ $1.76 = _____ cents

⑬ 243 cents = $ ___.___   ⑭ $0.54 = _____ cents

NOTE TO HOME
Students change dollars to cents and cents
to dollars.

Unit 4   Lesson 148 • **333**

Copyright © SRA/McGraw-Hill

◆ **LESSON 148** Adding and Subtracting Money

Solve these problems.

15 How many cents do the doll and the hat cost all together?

DOLL
$6.50

650¢ + 75¢ = _____¢

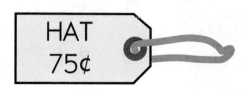

HAT
75¢

16 Leslie has $9.

Suppose she buys the doll and the hat.

How much change will she get?

```
  900¢
− 725¢
```

900¢ − 725¢ = _____¢

17 How long are both tables together? _____ cm

```
 181
+181
```

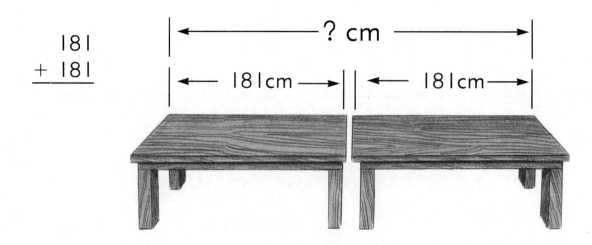

? cm

← 181cm → ← 181cm →

NOTE TO HOME
Students solve problems
involving money and measurement.

334 • Money and Multiplication

LESSON 149

Name _____

Adding and Subtracting with Three Digits

Solve these problems. Watch the signs.

1
$$\begin{array}{r} 291 \\ -\ 187 \\ \hline \end{array}$$

2
$$\begin{array}{r} 356 \\ +\ 294 \\ \hline \end{array}$$

3
$$\begin{array}{r} 869 \\ -\ 334 \\ \hline \end{array}$$

4
$$\begin{array}{r} 487 \\ +\ 202 \\ \hline \end{array}$$

5
$$\begin{array}{r} 125 \\ +\ 125 \\ \hline \end{array}$$

6
$$\begin{array}{r} 834 \\ -\ 78 \\ \hline \end{array}$$

7
$$\begin{array}{r} 63 \\ +\ 159 \\ \hline \end{array}$$

8
$$\begin{array}{r} 547 \\ -\ 123 \\ \hline \end{array}$$

9
$$\begin{array}{r} 425 \\ +\ 58 \\ \hline \end{array}$$

10
$$\begin{array}{r} 483 \\ +\ 108 \\ \hline \end{array}$$

11
$$\begin{array}{r} 737 \\ -\ 146 \\ \hline \end{array}$$

12
$$\begin{array}{r} 200 \\ -\ 183 \\ \hline \end{array}$$

13
$$\begin{array}{r} 728 \\ -\ 108 \\ \hline \end{array}$$

14
$$\begin{array}{r} 700 \\ -\ 243 \\ \hline \end{array}$$

15
$$\begin{array}{r} 65 \\ +\ 387 \\ \hline \end{array}$$

16
$$\begin{array}{r} 398 \\ -\ 127 \\ \hline \end{array}$$

NOTE TO HOME
Students practice mixed three-digit addition and subtraction problems.

◆ **LESSON 149** Adding and Subtracting with Three Digits

Solve these problems.

⑰ How many cents do the car and the airplane cost all together?

_____ ¢

$2.98

$4.98

⑱ Kim is 190 centimeters tall. Two years ago he was 172 centimeters tall. How much did he grow in the two years?

_____ cm

⑲ There are 365 days in 1998 and the same number in 1999. How many days are there in both years?

_____ days

⑳ Mel rode his horse 24 miles on Monday. He rode another 27 miles on Tuesday. How many miles did he ride all together?

_____ miles

NOTE TO HOME
Students solve word problems.

LESSON
150

Name _____

Practicing Addition and Subtraction

These problems are easier than they look.
Can you solve them in your head?

Add.

1 300 + 400 = _____

2 300 + 399 = _____

3 299 + 400 = _____

4 299 + 399 = _____

5 200 + 500 = _____

6 201 + 499 = _____

7 499 + 201 = _____

8 499 + 202 = _____

Subtract.

9 400 − 100 = _____

10 400 − 99 = _____

11 399 − 99 = _____

12 401 − 99 = _____

13 375 − 100 = _____

14 374 − 99 = _____

15 373 − 98 = _____

16 372 − 97 = _____

NOTE TO HOME
Students solve addition and subtraction
problems in their head.

◆ **LESSON 150** Practicing Addition and Subtraction

Take-Home Activity

Make 1000

GAME

Players:	Two
Materials:	Two 0–5 Number Cubes, two 5–10 Number Cubes, pencil, and paper

RULES

Leader: Choose and write down any number between 250 and 750. This will be the starting number.

Player: Your are going to get as close to 1000 as you can without going over 1000. Roll all four cubes and make a one-, two- or three-digit number. Add your number to the leader's number. If you roll a 10, roll again.

Leader: Roll all four cubes and make a number. Add your number to the starting number.

Winner: The winner of the round is the person who gets closest to 1000 without going over.

NOTE TO HOME
Students approximate and solve problems involving multidigit addition and subtraction.

LESSON
151

Name _____

Approximating Answers

Three answers are given for each problem.
Only one of the answers is correct. Put a
check mark under the correct answer.
Explain why your answers make sense.

①
```
    98
+ 103
```
101 201 301

②
```
   407
+ 398
```
605 705 805

③
```
   489
+ 312
```
599 701 801

④
```
   482
+ 312
```
694 704 794

⑤
```
   306
+ 247
```
453 503 553

⑥
```
   694
+ 156
```
750 800 850

⑦
```
   398
- 199
```
99 199 299

⑧
```
    98
- 21
```
67 77 87

⑨
```
   803
- 198
```
605 705 805

⑩
```
   507
- 208
```
299 399 499

⑪
```
   895
- 494
```
301 401 501

⑫
```
   1000
-  750
```
250 350 450

NOTE TO HOME
Students practice adding and subtracting mentally.

Unit 4   Lesson 151 • **339**

◆ **LESSON 151** **Approximating Answers**

Solve these problems.

13 Max has a $10.00 bill.
He will buy flowers for $1.98.
How much change should he get?
Ring the correct answer.

    $2.02 $8.02 $10.02

14 Karen earned $3.25 yesterday.
She earned $4.50 today.
How much did she earn in the two days?
Ring the correct answer.

    $6.05 $7.05 $7.75

89¢
a bunch

75¢
a pound

15 Jim has $5. Does he have
enough money to buy

2 pounds of strawberries? _____

3 bunches of grapes? _____

3 pounds of pears? _____

4 pounds of strawberries? _____

$1.79
a pound

NOTE TO HOME
Students solve word problems using
mental math.

340 • Money and Multiplication

◆ **LESSON 151** Approximating Answers

Name _____

Solve these problems. If you use a calculator,
you must push all the keys and signs shown.

16 10 + 10 + 10 + 10 + 10 = _____

17 20 + 20 + 20 + 20 + 20 = _____

18 300 + 200 = _____

19 300 + 199 = _____

20 299 + 199 = _____

Write C if you would use a calculator
to work these problems. Write N if you
would not. Then work each problem.

21 ( ) 75 + 25   = _____

22 ( ) 76 + 25   = _____

23 ( ) 5 + 5   = _____

24 ( ) 372 + 469 = _____

NOTE TO HOME
Students assess the difficulty of math problems.

◆ **LESSON 151 Approximating Answers**

GAME

Play the "Checkbook" game.

"Earn" means to add money to the balance.

"Pay" means to subtract money from the balance.

Date	Earn	Pay	Balance
Start			$1000
Totals			

NOTE TO HOME
Students play a game in which they keep a checkbook balance.

LESSON 152

Name _____

Counting by 100s and 1000s

Count up. Fill in the missing numbers.

1 | 4763 | 4764 | | | | 4768 |

2 | 5387 | 5388 | | | | 5392 |

3 | 996 | 997 | | | | 1001 |

4 | 2018 | 2019 | | | | 2023 |

5 | | | | 3100 | 3101 | 3102 |

Count down. Fill in the missing numbers.

6 | 4325 | 4324 | | | | 4320 |

7 | 3102 | 3101 | | | | 3097 |

8 | 2004 | 2003 | 2002 | | | 1999 |

NOTE TO HOME
Students learn to count through 10,000.

◆ **LESSON 152** Counting by 100s and 1000s

Count up or down. Fill in the missing numbers.

9

100	200				600

10

1000		3000	4000		6000

11

1000	1500	2000		3000	3500

12

4500	4000		3000	2500	2000

Write the missing numbers on each line.

13

1000   2000   4000   5000

14

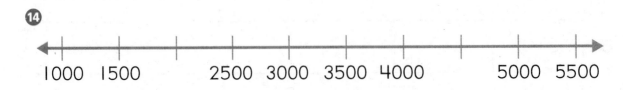

1000 1500   2500 3000 3500 4000   5000 5500

NOTE TO HOME
Students count by 100s and 1000s.

LESSON 153

Name _____

Adding Four-Digit Numbers

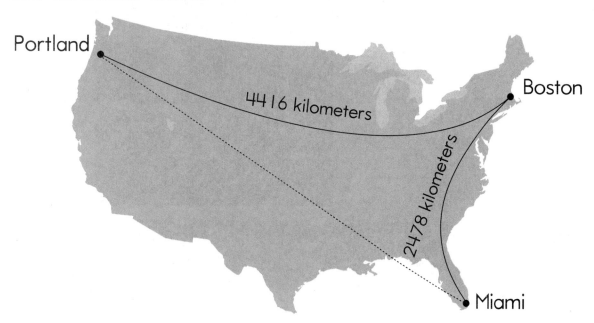

Use the map to answer the questions.

1 How many kilometers is it
from Portland to Boston? _____
from Boston to Miami? _____
from Portland to Boston to Miami? _____
from Miami to Boston to Portland? _____

2 About how many kilometers do you estimate it is from Miami
to Portland? _____

The National Basketball Association uses
over 1100 basketballs each season.

NOTE TO HOME
Students solve problems involving addition of
four-digit numbers.

◆ **LESSON 153** Adding **Four-Digit Numbers**

How well do you know
our first president?

Complete the chart
to show about
how old he was.

Event	Date	About how old?
❸ Born	1732	
❹ Married	1759	
❺ Became First President	1789	
❻ Re-elected President	1792	
❼ Died	1799	

❽ About how many years ago was George

Washington born? _____

Challenge: Find out more about George
Washington. Make a larger chart to show
how old he was when he did other things.

NOTE TO HOME
Students make calculations from a chart.

Name _____

Four-Digit Addition

Solve these problems.

	1 thousand		1 ten	
3587	3 thousands	5 hundreds	8 tens	7
+ 4605	+ 4 thousands	6 hundreds	0 tens	5
8192	8 thousands	1 hundred	9 tens	2

1
2356   ___ thousands ___ hundreds ___ tens ___
+ 4582   + ___ thousands ___ hundreds ___ tens ___

_____

2
3047   ___ thousands ___ hundreds ___ tens ___
+ 2659   + ___ thousands ___ hundreds ___ tens ___

GAME

Play the "Roll a Problem" game.

___ ___ ___ ___   ___ ___ ___ ___
+ ___ ___ ___ ___   + ___ ___ ___ ___

NOTE TO HOME
Students show how to add four-digit numbers.

◆ **LESSON 154 Four-Digit Addition**

Solve these problems.

③   2030
   + 3506

④   4278
   + 2356

⑤   3472
   + 5689

⑥   5555
   + 6666

⑦   9021
   + 6483

⑧   2500
   + 2500

⑨   8104
   + 5166

⑩   3047
   + 1099

⑪   4251
   + 4152

⑫   3300
   + 4711

NOTE TO HOME
Students practice adding four-digit numbers.

Name _____

Four-Digit Subtraction

Solve these problems. The first one has
been done for you.

1

$$
\begin{array}{r}
9 \\
2\ \cancel{10}\ 15\ 13 \\
\cancel{3}\cancel{0}\cancel{6}\cancel{3} \\
-\ 2\,5\,8\,4 \\
\hline
4\ 7\ 9
\end{array}
$$

	9 hundreds		
2 thousands	~~10~~ hundreds	15 tens	13
$\cancel{3}$ thousands	0 hundreds	$\cancel{6}$ tens	$\cancel{3}$
− 2 thousands	5 hundreds	8 tens	4
	4 hundreds	7 tens	9

2

$$
\begin{array}{r}
4783 \\
-\ 2651 \\
\hline
\end{array}
$$

___ thousands ___ hundreds ___ tens ___
− ___ thousands ___ hundreds ___ tens ___

3

$$
\begin{array}{r}
8074 \\
-\ 2356 \\
\hline
\end{array}
$$

___ thousands ___ hundreds ___ tens ___
− ___ thousands ___ hundreds ___ tens ___

4
$$
\begin{array}{r}
8525 \\
-\ 2475 \\
\hline
\end{array}
$$

5
$$
\begin{array}{r}
8943 \\
-\ 356 \\
\hline
\end{array}
$$

6
$$
\begin{array}{r}
7583 \\
-\ 2583 \\
\hline
\end{array}
$$

NOTE TO HOME
Students show how to subtract four-digit
numbers.

◆ **LESSON 155 Four-Digit Subtraction**

Solve these problems.

7 5000
    − 2500

8 4278
    − 2846

9 3472
    − 2333

10 3871
    − 2566

11 1478
    − 1185

12 7802
    − 4056

13 8222
    − 2550

14 7000
    − 4000

15 5310
    − 2173

16 4000
    − 1234

17 7456
    − 1435

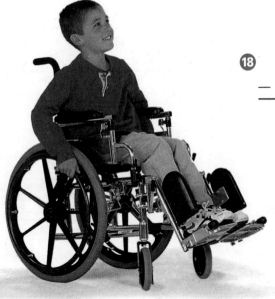

18 9412
    − 3571

19 2932
    − 1414

NOTE TO HOME
Students continue subtracting four-digit
numbers.

LESSON
156

Name _____

Keeping Sharp

Solve these problems. Watch the signs.

① 4653
+ 208

② 4653
− 208

③ 3489
− 2438

④ 846
+ 7259

⑤ 8000
− 2386

⑥ 6173
+ 3827

⑦ 4823
1759
+ 2427

⑧ 1958
66
+ 3471

⑨ 125
1625
2125
+ 3125

⑩ 1642
871
+ 2169

⑪ 2000
1776
+ 1492

⑫ 4952
3000
1586
+ 2

⑬ 2958
37
+ 416

⑭ 4821
2307
+ 219

⑮ 215
18
+ 4721

⑯ 400
30
+ 2

Play the "Four-Digit Addition" game.

NOTE TO HOME
Students add and subtract multiple digits.

Unit 4   Lesson 156 • **351**

◆ **LESSON 156 Keeping Sharp**

Suppose a wealthy person donated $8500 to your school to purchase playground equipment.

Complete the chart to show what you would buy. Make sure that you do not spend more than $8500.

Item	How many?	Total Price
Totals		

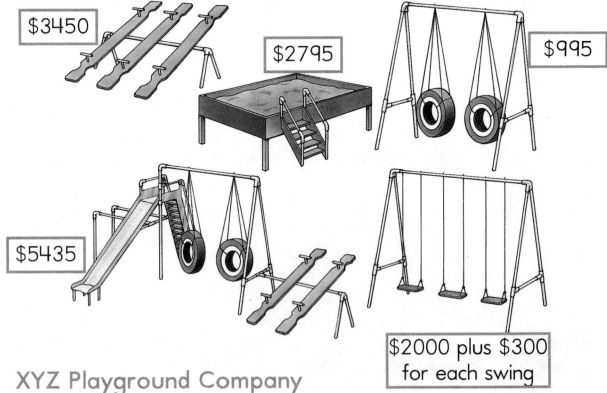

$3450

$2795

$995

$5435

$2000 plus $300 for each swing

XYZ Playground Company

All prices include shipping and setting up. Schools do not pay tax.

NOTE TO HOME
Students subtract and budget money.

Name _____

Applying Addition and Subtraction

SOCIAL STUDIES CONNECTION

Solve these problems.

① Antonio was born in 1994.
When will he be 95 years old? _____

② The United States was "born" in 1776.
When will the United
States be 250 years old? _____

③ Thomas Jefferson was born in 1743.
He died in 1826.
How old was he when he died?

_____ _____

How old would he be today? _____

NOTE TO HOME
Students solve four-digit word problems.

◆ **LESSON 157** Applying Addition and Subtraction

Solve these problems.

4 There are 1440 minutes
in one day.

How many minutes are there in two days? _____

How many minutes are there in three days? _____

5 Columbus discovered America in 1492.
How many years ago was that? _____

6 The Pilgrims first came to America in 1620. How
many years ago was that? _____

7 Mrs. Phillips wants to buy this car.
She has saved $4500. How
much more money does
she need?

$_____

$9457
tax included

GAME

Play the "Four Cubes
from 10,000 to 0" game.

NOTE TO HOME
Students solve four-digit problems.

LESSON

158

Name _____

Unit 4 Review

Solve these problems. Watch the signs.

Lessons
123–129

1 $8 + 4 =$ _____

2 $14 - 7 =$ _____

3 $8 + 7 =$ _____

4 $19 - 10 =$ _____

5 $8 + 9 =$ _____

6 $6 + 9 =$ _____

7 $5 +$ ☐ $= 13$

8 $10 =$ ☐ $+ 4$

9 ☐ $+ 7 = 15$

10 $9 +$ ☐ $= 17$

11 $5 \times 5 =$ _____

12 $4 \times 4 =$ _____

13 $15 \div 5 =$ _____

14 $3 \times 5 =$ _____

15 $8 \times 6 =$ _____

16 $12 \div 4 =$ _____

NOTE TO HOME
Students review unit skills and concepts.

Unit 4   Review • **355**

◆ **LESSON 158 Unit 4 Review**

Fill in the missing numbers.

Lesson **17**
152

59		61	62			65

18

896			899			902

19

5048			5051		5053

What is the right sign? Draw <, >, or =.

Lessons **20**   65 ◯ 56
152-154

21 972 + 4   ◯   952 + 4

22 8078 + 5   ◯   5 + 8078

23 541 + 5   ◯   541 + 10

NOTE TO HOME
Students review unit skills and concepts.

◆ **LESSON 158 Unit 4 Review**

Name _____

Solve these problems. Watch the signs.

Lessons   ㉔   29   ㉕   37   ㉖   595   ㉗   333
153–157   + 67   − 29   − 435   + 666

           ㉘   4072   ㉙   4072   ㉚   125   ㉛   461
               − 1286   + 1286   125   39
                                                  125   + 15
                                                + 125

㉜ Eight goldfish cost $2.
How much does each goldfish cost? _____¢

NOTE TO HOME
Students review unit skills and concepts.

◆ **LESSON 158 Unit 4 Review**

Solve these problems.

Lessons
153–157

㉝ Los Amigos School put on a play.
It gave two shows.
1255 tickets were sold on Monday.
1347 tickets were sold on Tuesday.
How many tickets were sold all together? _____

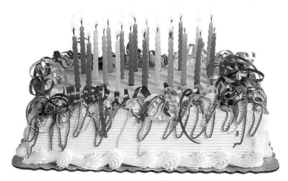

㉞ Eileen is seven years old.
How old will she be in 27 years? _____

7 cm

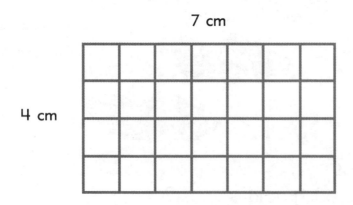

4 cm

Lesson
119

㉟ The area is _____ square centimeters.

NOTE TO HOME
Students review unit skills and concepts.

LESSON
159

Name _____

Unit 4 Test

ALGEBRA
READINESS

Check your math skills.
Solve these problems.

1 $16 - 7 =$ _____

2 $2 + 9 =$ _____

3 $14 - 9 =$ _____

4 $5 + 8 =$ _____

5 $8 + \boxed{} = 13$

6 $12 = \boxed{} + 4$

7 $\boxed{} + 7 = 12$

8 $11 = 5 + \boxed{}$

9 $5 \times 7 =$ _____

10 $9 \times 9 =$ _____

11 $6 \times 8 =$ _____

12 $2 \times 7 =$ _____

13 $7 \times 8 =$ _____

14 $10 \div 2 =$ _____

15 $3 \times 4 =$ _____

16 $24 \div 8 =$ _____

NOTE TO HOME
This test checks unit skills and concepts.

◆ **LESSON 159 Unit 4 Test**

Fill in the missing numbers.

⑰

77	78					83

⑱

296	297					302

⑲

5088	5089				5093

What is the right sign? Draw <, >, or =.

⑳   54 + 4   ◯   64 + 5

㉑   735   ◯   537

㉒   9025 + 1   ◯   9025 + 3

㉓   735 + 15   ◯   15 + 735

NOTE TO HOME
This test checks unit skills and concepts.

◆ **LESSON 159 Unit 4 Test**   Name _____

Solve these problems. Watch the signs.

㉔   28
    + 59

㉕   74
    − 69

㉖   973
    + 809

㉗   627
   − 438

㉘ 2483
  + 3567

㉙ 4076
  − 1284

㉚   25
    25
    25
  + 25

㉛ 2500
  2500
  2500
 + 2500

㉜   380
  4627
  1212
 + 400

㉝ Taro bought three stickers.
They cost 4¢ each. How much did
they cost all together? _____¢

◆ **LESSON 159   Unit 4 Test**

Solve these problems.

㉞ Anne bought seven colored pencils.
She paid 56¢.
How much did each pencil cost? _____¢

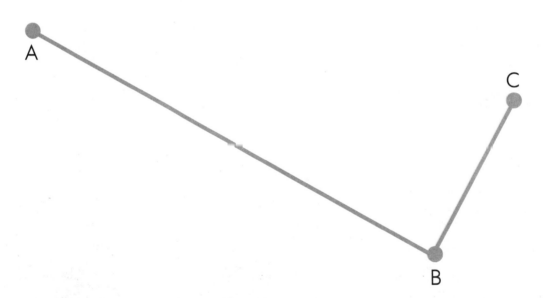

㉟ It is 3417 kilometers from A to B.
It is 1429 kilometers from B to C.
How far is it from A to B to C? _____ kilometers

NOTE TO HOME
This test checks unit skills and concepts.

LESSON **160**

Name _____

Extending the Unit

Multiply. Then use the code below to solve the riddle, "What should you do when an elephant breaks its toe?"

2 × 4	8	C
4 × 4		
4 × 3		
3 × 4		

2 × 2		
3 × 3		
5 × 4		

1 × 4		
2 × 3		
5 × 3		

4 × 1		
2 × 5		
1 × 3		
1 × 1		
5 × 5		

Code

1	3	4	6	8	9	10	12	15	16	20	25
C	U	T	O	C	H	R	L	W	A	E	K

NOTE TO HOME
Students practice multiplication facts as they solve a puzzle.

◆ **LESSON 160** **Extending the Unit**

Write the total number of steps you need
to take to reach the goal. If you will not
reach the goal, write N.

	Goal	First Two Steps	Total Steps
❶	20	0→2→4	
❷	20	0→5→10	
❸	197	0→2→4	
❹	200	0→5→10	

Solve.

❺ 3 + 3 + 3 + 3 + 3 + 3 = _____

❻ 6 + 6 + 6 = _____

❼ 6 × 3 = _____

❽ 3 × 6 = _____

❾ Ring the even numbers. Put a square around the
numbers divisible by 5.

23   45   16   30   0   9   14   200   197   63

NOTE TO HOME
Students explore multiplication,
addition, and division.

Name _____

Mixed Practice
Pages 1–10

Count up or count down. Fill in the missing numbers.

1 ____ 80 ____ 82   **2** 49 ____ ____ 52

3 18 ____ ____ 21   **4** 60 ____ ____ 57

How much money?

5 $_____

6 $_____

7 $_____

8 There are 30 days in April. Fill in the missing numbers.

April						
Sunday	Monday	Tuesday	Wednesday	Thursday	Friday	Saturday
		1	2	3	4	5

NOTE TO HOME
Students practice skills from pages 1–10.

Mixed Practice
Pages 1–20

❶ Write the number that comes after 69. _____

❷ Write the number that comes before 90. _____

Solve these problems.

❸   87
    − 3
    —————

❹   62
    + 2
    —————

❺   19
    − 3
    —————

❻   42
    + 0
    —————

❼ $7 + 9 =$ _____

❽ $9 + 4 =$ _____

❾ $6 + 5 =$ _____

❿ $3 + 8 =$ _____

Use play money to act out the stories.

⓫ I had $54.
I found $5 more.
How much money do I have now? $_____

⓬ I had $18.
I lost $3.
How much money do I have left? $_____

NOTE TO HOME
Students practice skills from pages 1–20.

Name _____

Mixed Practice
Pages 1–30

Solve these problems.

①   3
   + 8
_____

②   10
   + 5
_____

③   7
   + 8
_____

④   4
   + 6
_____

⑤   5
   + 4
_____

⑥ $6 + 8 =$ _____ $+ 6$

⑦ $9 + 6 = 6 +$ _____

⑧ $6 + 6 =$ _____

⑨ $8 + 9 =$ _____

⑩ $7 + 8 =$ _____

⑪ $4 + 6 =$ _____

⑫ $5 + 9 =$ _____

⑬ $7 + 7 =$ _____

⑭ Write the number before 71. _____

Solve. Write a number sentence.

⑮ There are six red balls and seven yellow balls. How many balls all together?

_____ + _____ = _____

⑯ Sheila had nine cents. Juan gave her five cents more. How much does she have now?

_____ + _____ = _____ ¢

NOTE TO HOME
Students practice skills from pages 1–30.

Mixed Practice
Pages 1–40

Solve these problems.

1 4
   + 6

2 8
   + 7

3 6
   + 9

4 8
   + 8

5 7
   + 5

6 8 − 6 = _____

7 9 − 3 = _____

8 12 − 0 = _____

9 7 − 4 = _____

10 6 + ☐ = 14

11 ☐ + 7 = 15

12 ☐ + 10 = 13

13 ☐ + 4 = 10

Solve.

14 Seven birds are on a wire.
    Four more land. How many birds now? _____

15 Two more birds land. How many now? _____

16 Six more land. How many birds now? _____

NOTE TO HOME
Students practice skills from pages 1–40.

Name _____

Mixed Practice
Pages 1–50

Solve these problems.

1 6 + 4 = _____

2 ☐ + 6 = 9

3 ☐ + 6 = 10

4 9 − 6 = _____

5 10 − 4 = _____

6 8 + ☐ = 16

7 10 − ☐ = 4

8 16 − 8 = _____

9   17
  − 8

10   12
  − 4

11   7
  − 3

12   14
  + 10

13   8
  − 4

Write a subtraction sentence to solve.

14 There are seven eggs. Four broke.
How many are eggs are left?

_____ − _____ = _____

15 Nine lights are on. Turn five off.
How many lights are on now?

_____ − _____ = _____

NOTE TO HOME
Students practice skills from pages 1–50.

Mixed Practice
Pages 1–60

❶ 12 − 9	❷ 11 − 6	❸ 18 − 9	❹ 14 − 5	❺ 13 − 6

❻ 10 − 6	❼ 15 − 10	❽ 17 − 8	❾ 12 − 11	❿ 15 − 9

⓫ 6 − 3 = _____   ⓬ 9 − 4 = _____

⓭ 16 − 7 = _____   ⓮ 11 − 7 = _____

Solve these problems.

⓯ You have 16 vases. Nine break.
How many vases are left? _____

⓰ There are 12 children. Five are girls.
How many are boys? _____

⓱ You bake 18 pies. Nine are hot.
How many are not hot? _____

⓲ You plant 15 rosebushes. One
does not grow. How many did? _____

NOTE TO HOME
Students practice the skills from pages 1–60.

Name _____

Mixed Practice
Pages 1–70

Use the graphs to answer the questions.

Students	😊 = 1 student
Group 1	😊 😊 😊
Group 2	😊 😊
Group 3	😊 😊 😊 😊 😊 😊

1. How many students are in group 2? _____

2. Which group has the most students? _____

3. How many more students are in
   Group 3 than in Group 1? _____ more

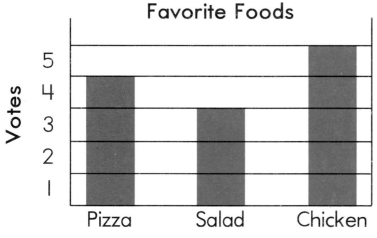

Favorite Foods

Votes: Pizza, Salad, Chicken

4. Which food got the most votes?

   _____

5. Which food got three votes?

   _____

6. How many votes for pizza? _____

NOTE TO HOME
Students practice skills from pages 1–70.

Mixed Practice
Pages 1–78

Use the graph to answer the questions.

Favorite Ice Cream Flavors

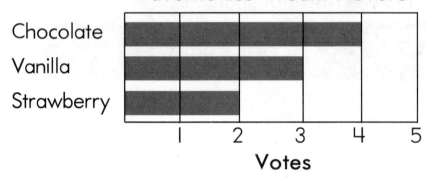

1 How many votes did chocolate get? _____

2 How many votes were there in all? _____

3 Which flavor got two votes? _____

How much money?

4 _____¢

5 $_____

Show this amount with coins.
Draw as few coins as you can.

6 43¢

NOTE TO HOME
Students practice skills from pages 1–78.

Name _____

Mixed Practice
Pages 1–90

How long? Measure.

1 _____ centimeters

2 _____ inches

3 About how long is it in real life?

☐ about 1 meter

☐ less than 1 meter

☐ more than 1 meter

First estimate in inches the length of each object.
Then measure to check.

4 Estimate about _____

Measure _____

5 Estimate about _____

Measure _____

NOTE TO HOME
Students practice skills from pages 1–90.

Mixed Practice
Pages 1–98

Name the object.

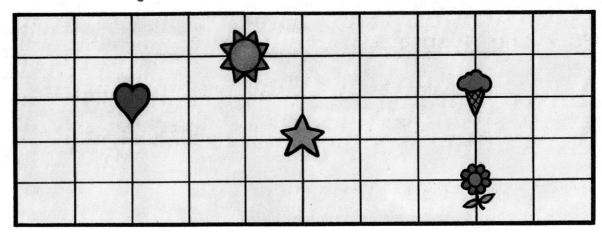

1 Four steps over and four steps up? _____

2 Eight steps over and three steps up? _____

Solve.

3
$$\begin{array}{r} 6 \\ +\,4 \\ \hline \end{array}$$

4
$$\begin{array}{r} 0 \\ +\,8 \\ \hline \end{array}$$

5
$$\begin{array}{r} 54 \\ +\,2 \\ \hline \end{array}$$

6
$$\begin{array}{r} 89 \\ -\,3 \\ \hline \end{array}$$

7
$$\begin{array}{r} 41 \\ -\,3 \\ \hline \end{array}$$

8 $6 + 5 - 2 =$ _____

9 $41 - 3 =$ _____

Solve these problems.

10 Pablo has $16. He buys a game
for $9. How much does he have left? _____

11 Carla has $9. Pens cost $4.
Can she buy two pens? _____

NOTE TO HOME
Students practice skills from pages 1–98.

Name _____

Mixed Practice
Pages 1–110

Write the standard name for each of these.

1 8 tens and 12 = _____   **2** 3 tens and 14 = _____

Use sticks or other objects to solve.

3 42 + 26 = _____   **4** 35¢ + 17¢ = _____¢

Use sticks to add. Write what you did.

5 24   _____ tens and _____
    + 17   + _____ tens and _____
             _____
              _____ tens and _____

Add.

6 24   **7** 19   **8** 25   **9** 31
    + 47   + 13   + 25   − 14

10 72   **11** 29   **12** 77   **13** 41
     + 19   + 7   + 77   + 13

NOTE TO HOME
Students practice skills from pages 1–110.

Mixed Practice
Pages 1–120

Use the table. Solve the problems.

Number of 2nd Graders		
Class	Boys	Girls
A	15	17
B	12	19
C	21	9

① How many children in class B? _____

② How many girls are in A and C all together? _____

Rewrite to show more units.

③ 17 = _____ tens and _____   **④** 52 = _____ tens and _____

Solve.

⑤ 74   **⑥** 32   **⑦** 68   **⑧** 24   **⑨** 15
   + 18   + 32   + 14   + 36   − 8

Solve these problems.

⑩ There are 11 flowers. Six are pink.
How many are not pink? _____

⑪ You have 12 cups. Four break.
How many cups are left? _____

NOTE TO HOME
Students practice skills from pages 1–120.

Name _____

Mixed Practice
Pages 1–130

Use sticks or other objects to subtract.

❶ 100   **❷** 90   **❸** 40   **❹** 20   **❺** 30

    −60   −70   − 0   −10   −20

Use sticks to help. Write what you did.

❻ 60 − 27 = _____   _____ tens and _____

                              − _____ tens and _____

                                _____ tens and _____

❼ 90 − 25 = _____   _____ tens and _____

                              − _____ tens and _____

                                _____ tens and _____

Solve these problems.

❽ 60   **❾** 40   **❿** 84   **⓫** 19   **⓬** 45

    −29   −37   −49   −12   −13

NOTE TO HOME
Students practice skills from pages 1–130.

Mixed Practice
Pages 1–140

Solve.

1. 65
   −39

2. 21
   −12

3. 19
   −18

4. 71
   −54

5. 55
   −10

6. 56
   −30

7. 80
   −15

8. 23
   −19

9. 92
   −29

10. 70
    −19

Solve these problems.

11. Leroy has $47. Sara has $62.
    How much less money
    does Leroy have than Sara? $_____ less

12. Janell is 60 inches tall.
    Steven is 12 inches
    shorter. How tall is Steven? _____ inches

Add.

13. 73
    +42

14. 45
    +25

15. 46
    + 39

16. 64
    +17

17. 70
    +18

18. 63
    +27

19. 32
    +18

20. 50
    + 25

21. 29
    +23

22. 13
    +56

NOTE TO HOME
Students practice skills from pages 1–140.

Name _____

Mixed Practice
Pages 1–150

What time is it?

1

quarter after _____

half past _____

quarter to _____

2

quarter after _____

half past _____

quarter to _____

Draw the hands.

3 2:00

4 9:30

Solve these problems. Watch the signs.

5
```
  43
- 27
```

6
```
  43
+ 27
```

7
```
  37
+ 54
```

8
```
  90
- 17
```

9
```
  64
- 25
```

10
```
  39
+ 45
```

NOTE TO HOME
Students practice skills from pages 1–150.

Mixed Practice

Pages 1–158

What time is it?

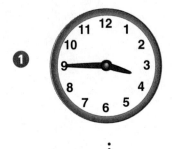

1

_____ : _____

2

_____ : _____

Draw the hands.

3 6:45

4 4:15

Color one quarter $\left(\dfrac{1}{4}\right)$ of each figure.

5

6

7

Color two thirds $\left(\dfrac{2}{3}\right)$ of each figure.

8

9

10

380 • Mixed Practice

NOTE TO HOME
Student practice skills from pages 1–158.

Name _____

Mixed Practice

Pages 1–170

What fraction is shaded?

1 _____

2 _____

What fraction of the set is blue?

3 _____

4 _____

Complete the chart. Use play coins to help.

Make this amount.	Use this kind of coin.	How many coins?
5 $1	quarters	
6 50¢	nickels	

Name the figures.

7 1 _____

8 2 _____

9 1 _____

10 2 _____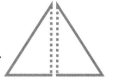

NOTE TO HOME
Students practice skills from pages 1–170.

Mixed Practice
Pages 1–178

Which are the same shape and size?
Circle your answer.

1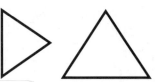

2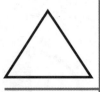

Draw as many lines of symmetry as you can.

3   **4**   **5**   **6**

Draw a line to match the space figure.

7 cone •

8 sphere •

9 rectangular prism •

 NOTE TO HOME
Students practice skills from pages 1–178.

Name _____

Mixed Practice
Pages 1–186

Complete the chart. Use patterns to help.

0	1	2	3	4	5	6	7	8	9
10		12							
							27		
			33						
				44					
					55				
						66			
	91								99

NOTE TO HOME
Students practice skills from pages 1–186.

Mixed Practice
Pages 1–190

Write the rule.

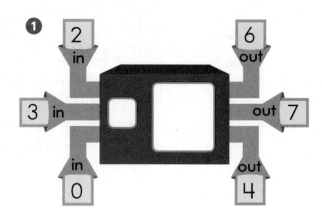

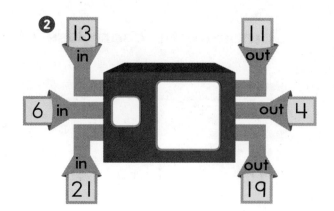

What temperature?

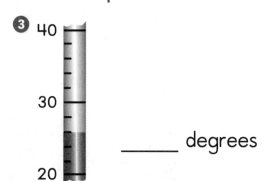

_____ degrees

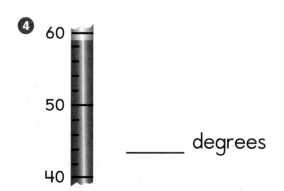

_____ degrees

What time is it?

_____ : _____

_____ : _____

NOTE TO HOME
Students practice skills from pages 1–190.

Name _____

Mixed Practice
Pages 1–208

What is the right sign? Draw <, >, or =.

1 25−4 ☐ 25−2   **2** 12 + 5 ☐ 12 + 9

About what time is it? Tell the time to the nearest half hour.

3    **4**    **5**

_____ : _____   _____ : _____   _____ : _____

Draw the minute hands.

6    **7**    **8**

2:24   5:56   7:07

Solve these problems.

9 26   **10** 18   **11** 73   **12** 59   **13** 86
  + 26   + 27   + 14   − 7   − 39

NOTE TO HOME
Students practice skills from pages 1–208.

Mixed Practice
Pages 1–220

Complete the chart. Use the map to find the shortest distances. Answer the questions.

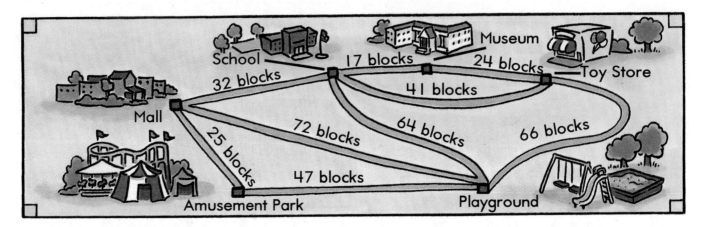

		Shortest Distance
❶	mall to museum	
❷	museum to playground	
❸	school to toy store	

❹ What is farthest from the mall? _____

❺ What is farthest from the toy store? _____

❻ What is the shortest way from the mall to

the toy store? _____

_____

NOTE TO HOME
Students practice skills from pages 1–220.

Name _____

Mixed Practice
Pages 1–230

What is the right sign?
Draw < , >, or =.

Is it possible to
make a triangle?

1 4 + 5 ◯ 6   yes   no

2 5 + 6 ◯ 12   yes   no

Add. Then circle all the odd numbers.

3 8 + 7 = _____   **4** 24 + 10 = _____

5 6 + 9 = _____   **6** 13 + 4 = _____

Ring each wrong answer. (Two of the
answers are wrong.)

7
$$46 \\ + 37 \over 74$$

8
$$23 \\ - 14 \over 9$$

9
$$37 \\ + 28 \over 65$$

10
$$84 \\ - 17 \over 73$$

Add.

11
$$24 \\ 17 \\ + 36$$

12
$$77 \\ 14 \\ + 34$$

13
$$75 \\ 85 \\ + 90$$

14
$$76 \\ 82 \\ + 14$$

NOTE TO HOME
Students practice skills from pages 1–230.

Mixed Practice
Pages 1–240

How much does it weigh?

1

☐ about a pound

☐ less than a pound

☐ more than a pound

2

☐ about a pound

☐ less than a pound

☐ more than a pound

How much does it hold?

3

☐ about a gallon

☐ less than a gallon

☐ more than a gallon

4

☐ about a liter

☐ less than a liter

☐ more than a liter

 NOTE TO HOME
Students practice skills from pages 1–240.

Name _____

Mixed Practice
Pages 1–250

Round to the nearest ten.

① 54 _____   **②** 37 _____   **③** 96 _____   **④** 45 _____

Round to the nearest ten. Then add.

⑤ 84 + 27   **⑥** 54 + 91

_____ + _____ = _____   _____ + _____ = _____

Solve these problems.

⑦ Craig swam 50 feet across the pool. Robin swam the same distance. Then she swam 75 more feet.

How far did Robin swim? _____ feet

⑧ One dog weighs 54 pounds. The other dog weighs 48 pounds. About how many pounds do they weigh all together?

_____

⑨ Grandma is 72 years old. Little Hector is six years old. How much older is Grandma?

_____

NOTE TO HOME
Students practice skills from pages 1–250.

Mixed Practice
Pages 1–260

Fill in the missing numbers.

1

○○○ ○○○	○○○ ○○○	○○○ ○○○	○○○ ○○○	○○○ ○○○	○○○ ○○○	○○○ ○○○	○○○ ○○○
6	12	18			36		48

Solve these problems.

2 A video game costs $49. The video game
player costs $99. How much all together? $_____

3 Dora needs 85 cents. She has
47 cents. How much more does she need? _____¢

Solve these problems. Watch the signs.

4
```
   34
   46
+ 12
```

5
```
   50
   80
+ 30
```

6
```
   12
   91
+ 42
```

7
```
   19
   47
+ 78
```

8
```
   78
- 43
```

9
```
   40
- 16
```

10
```
   25
-  2
```

11
```
   91
-  8
```

NOTE TO HOME
Students practice skills from pages 1–260.

Name _____

Mixed Practice
Pages 1–270

How many?

1 4 × 3 = _____

2 6 × 4 = _____

Find the area.

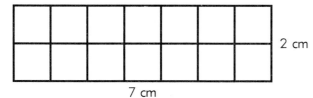

2 cm

7 cm

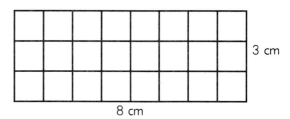

3 cm

8 cm

3 The area is _____
square centimeters.

7 × 2 = _____

4 The area is _____
square centimeters.

8 × 3 = _____

Solve these problems.

5 Pencils are 8 cents each.
How much are four pencils? _____ cents

6 Five students each carry four books.

How many books? _____

NOTE TO HOME
Students practice skills from pages 1–270.

Mixed Practice
Pages 1–280

Use cubes or sticks to solve these problems.

1 Take 15 cubes. Divide them into five groups.
How many cubes in each group? _____ $5 \times \boxed{} = 15$

2 Take 20 cubes. Divide them into five groups.
How many cubes in each group? _____ $5 \times \boxed{} = 20$

3 Roll a 0–5 Number Cube 20 times. Fill in the chart.

Number	Tallies	Totals
0		
1		
2		
3		
4		
5		

Solve this problem.

4 One book costs $4.
How much do three books cost? $_____

How much do five books cost? $_____

NOTE TO HOME
Students practice skills from pages 1–280.

Name _____

Mixed Practice
Pages 1–290

Use coins or objects to act these out in a group.

1 Fourteen cents are to be divided equally between two children. How many cents for each child?

$$14 \div 2 = \underline{\hspace{2cm}}$$

2 Twenty-one cents are to be divided equally among three children. How many cents for each child?

$$21 \div 3 = \underline{\hspace{2cm}}$$

Complete the chart.

Today is Monday.

Number of days	Day it was	Day it will be
1		
3		
6		
7		

NOTE TO HOME
Students practice skills from pages 1–290.

Mixed Practice • **393**

Copyright © SRA/McGraw-Hill

Mixed Practice
Pages 1–300

Solve these problems.

1

2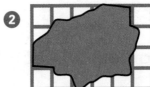

How many units long? _____

How many units long? _____

Write two number sentences that give the number shown as an answer.

3   _____ ÷ _____ = 9   _____ ÷ _____ = 9

4   _____ ÷ _____ = 7   _____ ÷ _____ = 7

Solve these problems. Use shortcuts if you can.

5 4 + 2 + 1 + 6 + 3 + 7 = _____

6 9 + 1 + 3 + 6 + 4 + 2 + 8 = _____

What is the rule?

7
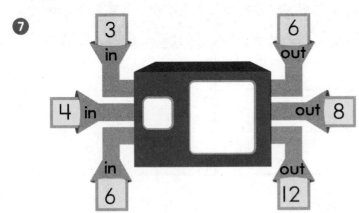

NOTE TO HOME
Students practice skills from pages 1–300.

Name _____

Mixed Practice
Pages 1–310

Fill in the missing numbers.

❶ (885 | 884 | | | 881 | | | | 877)

Write the correct number in each blank.

❷ 3 tens and 17 = _____ tens and _____

❸ 4 tens and 7 tens = _____ hundreds and _____ ten

Rewrite the problem. Then solve.

❹ 425   _____ hundreds and _____ tens and _____ ones
   + 157 + _____ hundreds and _____ tens and _____ ones
   _____
           _____ hundreds and _____ tens and _____ ones

NOTE TO HOME
Students practice skills from pages 1–310.

Mixed Practice
Pages 1–320

Add.

1   563
      + 474

2   748
      + 257

3   903
      + 487

4   327
      + 495

Subtract.

5   400
      − 212

6   750
      − 607

7   607
      − 418

8   298
      − 143

Rewrite to show more tens.

9 431 = _____ hundreds and _____ tens and _____

10 752 = _____ hundreds and _____ tens and _____

Solve these problems.

11 A television costs $400. Ramón has $275.
How much more does he need to buy the T.V.?

$_____

12 There are 342 students in the school.
There are 157 boys. How many are girls?

_____

NOTE TO HOME
Students practice skills from pages 1–320.

Name _____

Mixed Practice
Pages 1–330

Solve these problems quickly. Watch the signs.

①
```
  600
- 200
```

②
```
  600
+ 200
```

③
```
  700
- 400
```

④
```
  500
- 300
```

Solve these problems. Watch the signs.

⑤
```
  497
- 384
```

⑥
```
  900
- 472
```

⑦
```
  384
- 144
```

⑧
```
  807
+ 139
```

Solve.

⑨ How much do the juice and milk cost all together? _____¢

⑩ How much more does the juice cost than the milk? _____¢

Milk
$2.99

Juice
$3.49

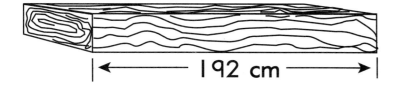
|←——— 192 cm ———→|

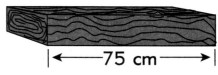
|←—75 cm—→|

⑪ How long are both planks together? _____ cm

NOTE TO HOME
Students practice skills from pages 1–330.

Mixed Practice
Pages 1-340

Ring the correct answer. Try to find each correct answer using mental math.

①
$$97$$
$$+\,204$$

101   201   301

②
$$407$$
$$+\,358$$

865   765   755

③
$$702$$
$$-\,198$$

504   604   704

Count up or count down. Fill in the missing numbers.

④

2762	2761			2758	

⑤

3998	3999			4002	4003

Fill in the boxes.

⑥   100   200   300   ☐   500   ☐

⑦   1000   ☐   ☐   4000   5000

Add.

⑧
$$3572$$
$$+\,4109$$

⑨
$$5074$$
$$+\,6181$$

⑩
$$3500$$
$$+\,3500$$

NOTE TO HOME
Students practice skills from pages 1–340.

Name _____

Mixed Practice
Pages 1–350

Solve these problems.

1   4285   _____ thousands _____ hundreds _____ tens _____
      + 5609   + _____ thousands _____ hundreds _____ tens _____
      _____   _____ thousands _____ hundreds _____ tens _____

2   7063   _____ thousands _____ hundreds _____ tens _____
      − 1245   − _____ thousands _____ hundreds _____ tens _____
      _____   _____ thousands _____ hundreds _____ tens _____

Solve.

3 Neil Armstrong landed on the moon in
1969. How many years ago was that? _____

4 Henry was born in 1953.
He was married in 1981.
How old was he when he got married? _____

NOTE TO HOME
Students practice skills from pages 1–350.

Mixed Practice
Pages 1–356

Solve these problems. Watch the signs.

1.
```
   37
   49
 + 56
 ____
```

2.
```
  6000
 − 1430
 _____
```

3.
```
   21
   68
 + 12
 ____
```

4.
```
  5000
 − 1013
 _____
```

5. $3 \times 7 =$ _____   6. $15 \div 3 =$ _____   7. $6 \times 2 =$ _____

Solve.

8. There are 24 hours in one day.
How many hours in two days? _____

9. There are 365 days in one year.
How many days in two years? _____

10. Seven days in one week.
How many days in four weeks? _____

11. How old will you be in 2007? _____ years old

NOTE TO HOME
Students practice skills from pages 1–356.

A

addition sentence
    4 + 1 = 5

area

C

circle

cone
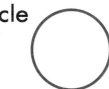

commutative property
    2 + 3 = 5
    3 + 2 = 5

congruent

cube

D

difference
    10 − 5 = 5

F

fraction
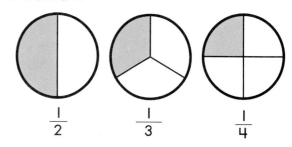

$\frac{1}{2}$ $\frac{1}{3}$ $\frac{1}{4}$

function machine

G

greater than
46 > 12

L

less than
10 < 65

N

number cube

number line
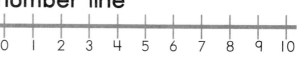

number strip

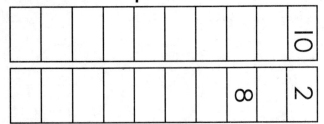

parallelogram

pattern

perimeter

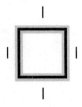

R

rectangle

S

sphere

square

subtraction sentence

$$5 - 1 = 4$$

sum

$$4 + 2 = 6$$

symmetry

T

tally marks

triangle